Tyne & Wear

Edited by Steph Park-Pirie

Young Writers
First published in Great Britain in 2004 by:
Young Writers
Remus House
Coltsfoot Drive
Peterborough
PE2 9JX
Telephone: 01733 890066
Website: www.youngwriters.co.uk

SB ISBN 1 84460 484 5

Foreword

Young Writers was established in 1991 and has been passionately devoted to the promotion of reading and writing in children and young adults ever since. The quest continues today. Young Writers remains as committed to engendering the fostering of burgeoning poetic and literary talent as ever.

This year's Young Writers competition has proven as vibrant and dynamic as ever and we are delighted to present a showcase of the best poetry from across the UK. Each poem has been carefully selected from a wealth of *Once Upon A Rhyme* entries before ultimately being published in this, our twelfth primary school poetry series.

Once again, we have been supremely impressed by the overall high quality of the entries we have received. The imagination, energy and creativity which has gone into each young writer's entry made choosing the best poems a challenging and often difficult but ultimately hugely rewarding task - the general high standard of the work submitted amply vindicating this opportunity to bring their poetry to a larger appreciative audience.

We sincerely hope you are pleased with our final selection and that you will enjoy *Once Upon A Rhyme Tyne & Wear* for many years to come.

Contents

The Poems

Pink Is For . . .

I like a pink pig
That has a wink and a blink
I like a rose
That I smell with my nose
I like a sunset
And it is fun
My mam puts pink
Lipstick on
I've a pink chocolate box
But I ate all the chocolates
I have a pink shell and I can hear the sea
I have a pink cozzie that I wear in the sea
I had a pink vase which I liked the best
But I threw it on Mars and I needed a rest.

Courtney Goulden (7)

Mrs Livesley

Mrs Livesley
Our headteacher is nice,
She sorts our school trips.
When she gets mad she is hot as spice,
When she is kind she is cool as ice.
She sometimes does an RE lesson with us,
Makes phone calls to our parents,
Sorts people who are in real big trouble,
At the end of the day they are glad,
But the very next day they are in real big trouble again.

Beth Micham (9)
Albert Elliott Primary School

Mr Collins

Mr Collins
Our teacher is nice,
He teaches us
About mice.
Mr Collins says some of us are bad,
But he says they're normally the lads.
He checks our work,
He sets it out,
All day long,
Just for us!

Amy Grieve (8)
Albert Elliott Primary School

Mr Wilson

Mr Wilson
Our caretaker is tall,
He can see over a wall
To get our ball.
He washes the doors
And sweeps the floor,
He makes the toilets clean,
To make them shine,
Ready for the next day,
So we have a clean school.

Colleen Caffrey (10)
Albert Elliott Primary School

Mr Collins

Mr Collins
Our teacher is nice,
He likes to eat
Curry and rice.
He is very tall,
He can reach the top of the wall,
He does the register,
He does naughty letters home
And he shouts when we are noisy
And he likes to teach.

Laura Bardwell (10)
Albert Elliott Primary School

Mrs Ghent

Mrs Ghent
Our kind helper,
When it's raining,
She helps us get shelter.
If people fall over hard
She takes them indoors, away from the yard.
She looks after the children,
She helps in the dinner hall,
She helps us with our work,
Mrs Ghent, our kind helper.

Roxy Moffat (9)
Albert Elliott Primary School

Mrs Livesley

Mrs Livesley
Our headteacher is cool,
Her special job
Is to run the school.
She sorts out files
And puts paper into piles.
On Wednesday night
She organises choir
And tells the children to behave,
At the end of the day
She sends them home.

Summer Phillipson (8)
Albert Elliott Primary School

Mrs Livesley

Mrs Livesley
Our headteacher is nice,
When we are hurt she puts on some ice,
Reading stories in the hall,
She is not very tall,
Helping us learn,
Teaching us RE,
Watching us sing,
Talking to visitors.

Leanne Coffer (10)
Albert Elliott Primary School

Mr Wilson

Mr Wilson
Our caretaker is tall,
So he can look
Over a wall.
He will call
If he sees someone's ball.
He goes up a ladder,
Upon the roof,
Cleans the school
And cleans the roof.

David Robertson (10)
Albert Elliott Primary School

Mrs Livesley

Mrs Livesley
Our headteacher is very busy,
But she does not like pop that's very fizzy,
She likes to have a drink of coffee,
Sometimes with it she has some toffee.
If you're naughty, she tells you off,
She's the one who rules the school.
She usually works in the office
And takes assembly.

Rebecca Morris (8)
Albert Elliott Primary School

Mrs Ghent

Mrs Ghent
Our helper in the class,
She'll always work with you
And help you to pass.
She works hard and is very busy,
She works hard and even gets dizzy.
Doing computer work,
Putting things into the photocopier,
Being a good dinner lady
And keeping watch for trouble at playtimes.

Ben Dunbar (8)
Albert Elliott Primary School

Mrs Snowdon

Mrs Snowdon
She's really kind,
She looks after children and she's got a good mind
And plays with them too,
Tells them what to do.
She is a lovely teacher,
She has got lots of friends
And she's happy all the time,
She's the nursery teacher.

Andrew Tate (8)
Albert Elliott Primary School

Mr Collins

Mr Collins
Our teacher is real cool,
Sometimes he's fun, but
Sometimes he's cruel.
When sorting things out,
He really needs to shout,
He teaches football and PE,
He always drinks coffee or tea,
He's really athletic and supportive,
He's really sweet
And gives us a bit of a treat,
But he's our Year 4/5 teacher.

Natalie Lindsay-Bewick (10)
Albert Elliott Primary School

Mr Wilson

Mr Wilson
Our caretaker is nice,
He picks up the rubbish
And gets rid of the mice.
On Tuesday night
He organises football,
He is tall to fix
The lights.

Michael Wilson (9)
Albert Elliott Primary School

What's That Noise?

What is that noise I hear over there?
It sounds like it's coming from behind the chair,
Is it a snake or is it a bear
Waiting to pounce and give me a scare?
Is it big?
Is it small?
Is it short?
Is it tall?
Is it thin?
Is it fat?
Will it have a friendly chat?
I wonder what it will wear?
What colour is its hair?
I know I should not give a care,
But I want to know what that noise is over there!

Jonathan Martin (10)
Bede Burn Primary School

The Shipwreck

The shipwreck,
Lost for eternity, buried in the seabed,
Rusted, ghostly, mysterious,
Like the lost city of Atlantis,
A watery grave for sailors,
It makes me curious,
Like an Agatha Christie mystery,
The shipwreck,
Sculpted there by Neptune in his great palace.

Rebecca Green (10)
Bede Burn Primary School

The Dancing Stars

Stars are dancers,
Jumping through the sparkling curtain sky,
They do the splits,
Then do high kicks,
So high it's over their heads.

They twinkle in the moonlight,
On the big bright stage,
Everybody claps as they dance,
They take a bow and skip off.

Next, on comes another star,
Shimmering and prancing around,
Of course it's her who we've been looking for -
The cheerleader.

Emma Hardy (10)
Bede Burn Primary School

The Angel Of The North

The Angel of the North,
Great metal structure, standing tall,
Rusty, ginormous, proud,
Like a pencil reaching for the sky,
Like a giant gazing over the land.
It makes me feel tiny,
Like a mouse – very small.
The Angel of the North,
Guarding the A1.

Shauni Mankin (10)
Bede Burn Primary School

Horrid Teachers

Ten horrid teachers worked down the mine,
One suffocated and then there were nine.

Nine horrid teachers forgot their bait,
One starved and then there were eight.

Eight horrid teachers wished they were in Heaven,
One fell off a cloud and then there were seven.

Seven horrid teachers bought a pick 'n' mix,
One choked and then there were six.

Six horrid teachers needed to be revived,
One stayed unconscious and then there were five.

Five horrid teachers slept on the floor,
One was trampled on and then there were four.

Four horrid teachers needed a wee,
One was sucked down the toilet and then there were three.

Three horrid teachers heard a loud moo,
One ran away and then there were two.

Two horrid teachers swam in the Don,
One drowned and then there was one.

One horrid teachers married a man called Ron,
They ran away together and then they were all gone!

Olivia Shaw (10)
Bede Burn Primary School

The Stars

The stars glisten across the big sky
And they sparkle,
They are gold stars that
Twinkle across the sky,
They go back in at dawn.

Sian O'Neil (8)
Bede Burn Primary School

Sweet Town

I wish our town was made of sweets,
Because it would be very neat.

Rice paper windows,
Chocolate bar doors,
Lollipop lampposts,
Peppermint rock floors.

Candy cane railings,
Sarsaparilla stalls,
Treacle toffee paving stones,
Liquorice allsort walls.

Marshmallow clouds,
Dolly mixture flowers,
Candyfloss trees,
Ice cream cone towers.

But it's only a wish and it won't come true,
Should I share my wish with you?

Alex Chaplin (11)
Bede Burn Primary School

Summer Holiday

The shiny hot sun
Glitters all day,
Goes at night.
It comes along on
My summer holiday.
It followed me to
The monkey bars and
It followed me home,
But then the moon
Came out and covered
The sun whole!

Rebecca May (8)
Bede Burn Primary School

Ten Cats

Ten furry cats sitting in a line,
One went away and then there were nine.
Nine furry cats eating from a plate,
One was sick and then there were eight.
Eight furry cats moved to Devon,
One came back home and then there were seven.
Seven furry cats hiding in Gran's knicks,
One was gassed and then there were six.
Six furry cats singing live,
One forgot his words and then there were five.
Five furry cats waiting at the door,
One was fed up and then there were four.
Four furry cats wanting their tea,
One was starved and then there were three.
Three furry cats desperate for the loo,
One couldn't wait and then there were two.
Two furry cats were chucked in the River Don,
One couldn't swim and then there was one.
One furry cat, his name was John,
He suddenly died and then there were none.

Bethany Carr (11)
Bede Burn Primary School

The Sun

The sun looks like a golden ball,
Shining on the dew-drenched grass.
It is early morn
And the sun is like a big one pound coin,
Way up above the clouds.
Just before the cock crows,
All the birds take flight,
To scrounge for food,
Stretching their wings after a good night's sleep.

Josie Miller (9)
Bede Burn Primary School

Why Me?

I sit and stare,
Standing all alone,
I've just escaped,
I wish I was home.

I wish they'd find
Someone new,
Finally into school,
Out here alleys are few.

I try my best,
'Cause I want to go somewhere,
But still they laugh and jeer,
They just don't care.

Lies and deception,
Oh, the pain never ends,
They treat me like nothing,
Though once they were my friends.

I don't wanna be great,
I don't wanna be grand,
I don't wanna be known all over this land,
I know I've got talent, I know it's true,
But they won't let it shine through.

Heather Robinson (11)
Bede Burn Primary School

The Sun

The sun shines up to the sky
People think how nice it is,
It's like a sunflower,
Glistening up to the big blue sky,
It's like an aeroplane flying.

Matthew Wood (9)
Bede Burn Primary School

The Moon

The most fabulous thing in the whole world,
On the beach seeing sunset,
Oh my goodness,
No one can argue with this.

Out your window,
Red and orange,
Beautiful sight,
In the night.

In your bed,
Looking out into the inky blue,
So sad to see the . . .
Wonderful sight go away from you.

Jack Davies (9)
Bede Burn Primary School

The Stars

Stars twinkle so bright,
They shimmer, shimmer like
Scattered sugar in the night.
The stars will never give you a fright,
They're only there for a gorgeous sight.
Now these stars are shiny
Like a real-life sword,
'Now who put them there?'
Our master God,
Our master Lord.

Jennifer Parkins (9)
Bede Burn Primary School

Cat

Large, round, bright eyes
Staring at the dark night skies
Around the corner like a dart he flies
Listening to children's grumpy sighs

Through the garden it seeks to play
Creeping up behind its prey
Surely going to have its say
It likes to get its own way

Strolling along the silent street
His body cold and wet because of sleet
Strong claws on the end of his feet
Around the corner him and his prey shall meet.

Daniel Murray (10)
Bede Burn Primary School

Black Panther

A jet-black panther slick
And swift like a cat.
Eyes like the moon, slit in two,
I bet they are watching you.

Claws as deadly as razorblades,
Knife-like fangs ready to sink into flesh.
Fur, black and silky,
Fit for the finest king.
Paws as silent as a slug,
So watch out when a panther is about.

Lauren Scott (10)
Bede Burn Primary School

The Human Monkey

He swings like lightning from tree to tree,
Having fun like you and me.
A naughty monkey that can't be beat,
Always untidy, never neat.

Extremely funny, chattery too
And springy, like a kangaroo.
We children as you can see,
Have monkeys in us, yes siree,
My brother Jake especially.

Luke Overton (10)
Bede Burn Primary School

The Rat

Jumping, screeching, scurrying,
Fighting swiftly.
Red, sharp, beady eyes like a train's light,
With the rope flying at the back.
So fast no one can see.
Nails sharp as shark's teeth,
So white like a piece of paper.
Hideous, thin face - so scary.

Jonathan Ivory (9)
Bede Burn Primary School

Sky Soccer

As they fly through the air
They don't care
As long as they score
Their points become more, more, more
What's happened to the ball?
Can you see it at all?
The score is unknown, but
Hopefully it's a win for
All Stars United.

Jordan Williamson (10)
Bede Burn Primary School

My Guinea Pigs

G reat eater
U ntidy sleeper
I nteresting fluff ball
N osy squeaker
E xtremely cute
A dventurous rodent

P lump peeper
I ndependent creature
G rass cutter.

Andrew Sheffer (10)
Bede Burn Primary School

Little Monsters

Ten little monsters sitting under a branch of pines,
A cone hit one in the head and then there were nine.

Nine little monsters swinging on the gate,
One fell off and then there were eight.

Eight little monsters imagining they're in Heaven,
One fell off his cloud and then there were seven.

Seven little monsters collecting sticks,
One tripped and fell and then there were six.

Six little monsters playing near a beehive,
One was stung and then there were five.

Five little monsters playing knockey-nine-door,
One was grounded and then there were four.

Four little monsters out at sea,
One fell overboard and then there were three.

Three little monsters fighting for the loo,
One was flushed away and then there were two.

Two little monsters having lots of fun,
One laughed so much his sides split and then there was one.

One little monster eating his scone,
He died of poisoning and then there were none.

Nicole Coutts (11)
Bede Burn Primary School

Fox

Legs as fast as light,
Running through
The farmer's fields at night.
A hen comes into its sight,
Preparing for an easy fight.
He is full after his small meal,
The farmer's hen was easy to steal.

Scott Mathers (10)
Bede Burn Primary School

The Stars

The stars are soldiers
Marching through the thick black sky,
Fighting the darkness,
Minions of the moon, their leader.
They are marching around the galaxy,
Making space
A better place
By fighting the darkness.

Lee Riley (11)
Bede Burn Primary School

Lilac

What is lilac?
A strip in the rainbow, glistening in the sunlight,
Pale blossom peeping from tiny buds,
Starfish floating above the deep ocean floor,
Lavender swaying in the gentle breeze,
Long dangling beads around necks,
Warm woollen jumpers worn by children.
Lilac is my favourite colour!

Chloe Angus (8)
Bournmoor Primary School

Blue

What is blue?
Sharp scissors cutting paper into crystals,
A child's balloon being blown up,
A homework book with lots of pages,
A picture-covered wall,
A door which keeps opening and shutting,
Blue is my favourite colour!

Ryan Cooke (7)
Bournmoor Primary School

Autumn

Autumn is when
Leaves go red,
Brown, yellow, crimson and orange.
When the wind blows
The trees sway
And the leaves fall to the ground.
Animals
Making their way to warm places,
Shiny horse chestnuts,
In bright green shells.
Juicy, dark
Blackberries and cherries.
Sycamore seeds twirling,
In crisp autumn air.
The smell of blazing bonfires.
The crunch and crackle
Of leaves under stamping feet.

Nicola Garden (9)
Bournmoor Primary School

Autumn

Acorns
Scattered on crispy ground.
The leaves
Twirling in the vicious wind,
While the river
Swirls and crashes
Against the rocks.
The bare trees of autumn
Banging into each other
As little animals
Search for food.

Katie Moule (7)
Bournmoor Primary School

Autumn

Sycamore seeds on the ground,
All the leaves
Fluttering down.
Conkers
On the trees.
Dew
Sparkling on the grass.
Cherries and berries everywhere.
People
Picking all kinds of fruit.
Smelling the autumn air,
Eating a delicious pear.
Everyone enjoying Bonfire Night,
Smelling
The gasping smoke
From the fire.

Jordan Gibson (8)
Bournmoor Primary School

Autumn

Leaves are different colours,
They fly all over the countryside,
Then crackle and crumble.
Conkers
Have yellow silk inside,
Berries, acorns, nuts,
Falling from trees.
Ponds
Get full of leaves.
Squirrels and hedgehogs hibernate
In autumn.

Chelsie Davidson (7)
Bournmoor Primary School

Autumn

Autumn
Is the sound
Of crispy leaves crunching on the ground
Windy, rainy days
Sunny days
To pick up conkers
And skip them on the river
Autumn air
As it springs through your body
You can feel the breeze
Come towards you
And slap your face
The leaves crunch
When you stand on them
While you are walking
Through the forest.

Holly Young (7)
Bournmoor Primary School

The Sea

The sea crashes,
The sea roars,
Fish jump
From sharks' jaws.
Dolphins do tricks,
As clever as can be.
Coral waves as each fish passes by.
The sea crashes,
The sea roars,
As whirlpool spin
When fish
Swim.
Fish as fast as a lightning flash.

Luke Armstrong (8)
Bournmoor Primary School

Blue

What is blue?
A gleaming dolphin swimming below the sea,
Seals slipping on freezing ice,
Squishy, bursting berries on a bush,
Different shades in a shining sky,
Thin, narrow veins inside you,
The threatening, thrashing shark.
Blue is my favourite colour!

Meghan Cowey (8)
Bournmoor Primary School

Red

What is red?
The bright pencil case on your long table,
The cheerful flower making me smile as I pass,
The fast, speeding car,
The big swings in the park,
The warm, comfy scarf tucked around my neck,
The straight ruler as I underline the date.
Red is my favourite colour!

Lauren Garden (7)
Bournmoor Primary School

Red

What is red?
Bright cheerful roses making you smile,
Cheeks glistening in the light,
Fluffy robins' chests, feathers and beautiful,
Crabs sneaking and creeping up the beach,
A fire engine zooming along the road,
Autumn leaves crunching when people stand on them.
Red is my favourite colour!

Chloe Horn (7)
Bournmoor Primary School

September

Leaves, leaves everywhere.
Might be yellow
Might be brown.
This is the month
When autumn comes.
Everyone is happy
To smell the air
And pick nuts
And play conkers.

Callum Rutter (8)
Bournmoor Primary School

The Hedgehog

The hedgehog
Curls up,
Scared of people.
Brown,
Running through bushes,
Eating bugs.

Dean Bester (8)
Bournmoor Primary School

Autumn

Autumn
Is the season
To enjoy ourselves
By jumping in the leaves
Of yellow, brown, red and orange
We watch
Apples, pears
And berries grow.

Ryan Kendall (7)
Bournmoor Primary School

Green

What is green?
The grass, soft and furry,
The new buds, hard and little,
The grapes, juicy and round,
The lettuce, big and crunchy,
The trees, large and happy,
The grasshopper, big and lively,
The small, interesting picture book.
My favourite colour is green!

Rebecca Postill (8)
Bournmoor Primary School

Autumn

The fruit is sweet and soft
Juicy like a lemon
Crispy leaves
Coloured leaves that crunch
Apples and pears
Ripe on trees.

Rachel Storey (9)
Bournmoor Primary School

Black

What is black?
Black is the dark night sky,
Black is the sleek cat miaowing and purring,
Black is the witch gliding through the sky,
Black is the storm-cloud ready to burst,
Black is the statue standing tall,
Black is your coat, keeping you warm,
Black is the dead flower, drooping and sad.
Black is my favourite colour!

Cara Sawyer (7)
Bournmoor Primary School

Blue

What is blue?
Blue is the sea -
 that creeps up the shore.
Blue is the sky -
 that will last for evermore.
Blue is the school jumper -
 that I need to wear.
Blue is the eye -
 of the big scary bear.
Blue is the colour -
 of the giant whales.
Blue is the hue -
 of the lizard's scales.
Blue is my favourite colour!

Bethany Whittle (8)
Bournmoor Primary School

Sounds

I hate the sound of thunder banging,
 bees buzzing,
 my mam shouting!
But . . .
I love the sound of cats miaowing,
 dogs barking,
 music playing
 and crisp, crunching leaves.

Sophie Wright (7)
Bournmoor Primary School

My Best Season

Autumn is my best season,
I like jumping in the leaves.
Brown, red, yellow,
Colourful leaves.
I can find
Conkers and acorns,
Hedges full
Of tasty, juicy berries.
Rain falls gently
In autumn.

Deniz Yentur (8)
Bournmoor Primary School

Monster

Big black horns
And bright sparkling teeth.
Stamps like
A huge, nasty giant.
Laughs spitefully.
Stalks Monster Land
For birds,
To crunch their bones!

Meaghan Stewart (7)
Bournmoor Primary School

The Monster

Taking giant footsteps
It plays with six footballs
It uses a hamster to bath with
The monster cries and howls
As it babies
And frogs.

Cenedra Van Tonder (8)
Bournmoor Primary School

Ghost

This ghost
Travels at night,
Giving people a fright!
He drains life
And eats skin,
Puts the bones
In the bin.
Lives in
A haunted hose -
Just this ghost
And a tiny mouse!

Thomas Wright (8)
Bournmoor Primary School

World Peace

I wish for world peace,
No fighting, no harm,
I wish that we could all stay calm.

I wish for world peace,
No crying, no hurt,
So why do people treat them like dirt?

I wish for world peace,
No threatening, no wars,
So why can't we give them a life like yours?

I wish for world peace,
So please make it happen,
All they want is for peace in the world.

Hannah Simnett (11)
Brandling Primary School

My Goblin, Ned

I have a goblin called Ned
Who loves his little brown ted
He escapes from his cage
And Mum gets in a rage
And that's what he does
His favourite food is grass
Which he always eats when we pass
His colour is green
He's like a machine
And that's my goblin, Ned.

Lauren Morton (7)
Brandling Primary School

Thomas

Thomas is my brother
He is very funny
His favourite food is salad
He has got blue eyes
The colour of his hair is blond
He likes playing games
He dislikes sports.

Ben Morton (8)
Brandling Primary School

Ben

Ben likes salad
Ben likes pizza
Ben likes sleeping in the cat's bed
Ben is funny
He likes honey.

Michael Rath (7)
Brandling Primary School

True Love

I love my friend, she loves me too
And that is oh so very true
I buy her presents, to show her I care
I love to look at her long dark hair

She holds my hand, she soothes my heart
She says I'm cool, well that's a start
But one thing I must say and do
Is announce my love, my love for you.

Malik Kalimba (7)
Brandling Primary School

My Best Friend

Best friends stick together
No matter what comes their way
That's why I choose Melissa
Hear what I have to say
She's my best friend because she cares
She's my best friend because she's kind
She's my best friend because she's helpful
She's always on my mind.

Brittany Wymark (10)
Brandling Primary School

Favourite Thing Is Spending Money

Money, money, people always collect money,
People never forget to collect money,
Because money is money.

Amy Brown (11)
Brandling Primary School

My Family

Our family name is Wink
We like to swim, but sometimes sink
My family likes to have fun
And sometimes we have a chip bun
Zoe sometimes groans
And then moans
Ryan is sometimes silly
And I like to eat chilli
We have lots of pets
And sometimes they go to the vet's.

Kelsey Wink (7)
Brandling Primary School

Animals

I went into the forest and saw a fish in a dish
A frog on a log
A bat that was fat
A rat on a mat
A cat that was flat
Then I saw a dog in the fog
A whale that was for sale
And a shark that could bark!

Jonathan Graham (7)
Brandling Primary School

My Best Friend

My best friend is called Kylie
She is really friendly
I love her as a best friend
Because she is everyone's friend
She laughs and plays the day away
She has got lots of friends
But her best friend is me.

Stephanie Baldwin (10)
Brandling Primary School

My Best Friend

My best friend is called Kelsey
She has got a sister called Chelsea

We like to have a joke about
But not when my mam gives me a clout!

Kelsey has hazel eyes
And loves to eat mince pies

She is neat and tidy just like me
But not when boys falls between thee

We love to laugh and have girly chats
And we even love to try on hats.

Rachel McGuigan (7)
Brandling Primary School

My Best Friend

My best friend is so cute,
She is very happy,
Like a laughing fruit,
She smells of flowers,
She thinks she's got magical powers,
My best friend is the best.

Louise Eggington (10)
Brandling Primary School

School Dinners

School dinners, school dinners,
Hairs in chips, hairs in chips,
Sickly semolina, sickly semolina,
I feel sick,
Oops, too late I've done it on my plate!

David Walker (10)
Brandling Primary School

Seasons

Spring is the time of year
Those little seedlings appear.
Under a little quilt of soil,
A sunflower seed that just won't spoil.
Now He has risen from the tomb He lay,
The man as a boy, who lay in the hay.

Summer is the time of year
The little seedlings disappear.
Up pops a huge big flowers,
Growing an inch, hour by hour.
Everyone is having fun,
In the roasting, oven sun.

Autumn is the time of year,
The huge big flower disappears.
It bends over, as brown as a log,
It gets blown away and chewed by a dog.
The trees begin to lose their beauty,
They blow at the teacher on duty.

Winter is the time of year,
The treetops are extremely bare.
The beautiful flowers are there no more,
Even the hanging baskets beside my door.
You have to remember the baby boy,
Who brought to the world love and joy.

Peter Daniel Pharaoh (11)
Brandling Primary School

My Best Friends

My best friends are good
Some of them go in loads of moods
Every time I have like loads of food
Sometimes they wear a frown
They always turn it upside down.

Kiran Hayer (10)
Brandling Primary School

School

First day back,
I carry a sack.

Reading books,
They give me the spooks.

Having dinner,
I play with a spinner.

Doing my work,
I talk to Kirk.

Going home,
I read a poem.

That's what I do at school.

Kevin Watson (10)
Brandling Primary School

Leilani

My hamster Lielani is so small and cuddly
I bet her personality is very bubbly
Her favourite foods are apple and nuts
She decides which treats are for her
The dog from 'The Magic Roundabout' has similar fur
She runs in her ball and bashes into the walls
Her colours are tan and white
And her little eyes sparkle bright!
She fills her mouth full of food
And she's never in a mood
She's as fat as a bee and best of all she loves me!

Holly Teasdale-Baird (10)
Brandling Primary School

My Best Friends

My best friend is Kiran,
She loves to wear a ribbon.

My best friend is Shanice,
She loves quiet and peace.

My best friend is Aisha,
She is much nicer.

My best friend is Zaina,
She is an entertainer.

My best friends are Zaina, Aisha,
Shanice and Kiran!

Rebecca McGuigan (10)
Brandling Primary School

Teachers

Some teachers are weird
They look on top of your head
And if you're telling a lie they look into your eyes
So some teachers are weird.

Some teachers are weird when it comes to art
And when they make all the mess they leave it all to us
So some teachers are weird.

Some teachers are weird
When it comes to home time they give us extra, extra homework
That's why teachers are weird.

Aisha Kalimba
Brandling Primary School

Goldilocks And The Three Bears

Once upon a rhyme
There was a little crime

When people were going out
Goldilocks would go about

Snooping around their house
As quiet as a mouse

But then she met the three bears
A very sneaky pair

For when they saw the cottage
She smelt the luscious porridge

When she had eaten it all
She went into the hall

She needed a rest
So she took the best

She sat on the chairs
And broke Baby Bear's

She saw the two beds
Two of them were red

She chose Baby Bear's
She didn't even care

When Goldilocks was dreaming
It was a happy feeling

But then the bears got home
She's glad this is a poem

They gobbled her up
In one big gulp

And that's the end of that!

Demi Williamson (10)
Dunn Street Primary School

Cinderella

'Cinderella, you horrible stink,
Clean my dress and dye it pink.'

'I must go to the ball,
So remember to iron my shawl!'

'Can I come and see the prince?' Cindy cried.
'He'll probably be very, very ugly!' she lied.

'No you can't, you stupid brat!
You can stay here and scrub the mat!'

So off they slob,
While Cindy sobs.

Then in one giant gust,
Popped out small Pixie Dust!

Off Cindy went to see the handsome prince,
But he was so ugly that Cindy winced!

She turned and escaped through a gap,
Then she saw a good-looking chap!

Now the clock goes tick-tock,
Look, now it's twelve o'clock.

He pulled her dress, made by Claire
And left her in her underwear!

Then she's chased round the shops,
By two *very* handsome cops.

For running around in her knicks!
Running as fast as two ticks!

Then the cops follow a brand new trail
And lock the two sisters up in jail.

This may sound very weird,
But Cindy disappeared!

So where *had* Cinderella gone?
She might have gone to MK1!

Kelly Johnson (10)
Dunn Street Primary School

Goldilocks And The Three Bears

Once upon a rhyme,
Goldilocks committed a crime.

Three bears went for a stroll,
Except Baby Bear who went for a roll.

She crept in through the house,
She was as silent as a mouse.

Goldilocks saw three bowls of porridge,
I think she also used her knowledge.

Ha! And she ate all of them and I mean all of them,
The porridge was a treat because Baby Bear was ten.

She sat on a chair
And she heard a tear.

The chair broke,
'Oops!' she spoke.

Goldilocks went upstairs,
She decided to glare.

She saw three little beds,
She went to lie down for ten.

The three little bears came running back,
They ran round the house trying to attack.

Goldilocks ran to the door,
The big bear fell on the floor.

Big Bear said, 'Never come back again,
Or if you do you will be in pain!'

She said, 'Why can't you listen?'
But she got sent to prison!

Danielle Graney (10)
Dunn Street Primary School

The Three Little Pigs

Once upon a time
An ugly wolf planned a crime.

He was angry so he did a sniff,
3 little pigs gave off a whiff.

The pigs were hard as bricks,
One of them made their house out of sticks.

He was drooling like a lion
And the pig was crying.

He ate him up with a gulp,
The pig, which was plump.

Then he went to the next
And his muscles he flexed.

He got the next in a rush,
Which he was plum as a bush!

The last was the hardest but it wasn't the last,
When the wolf puffed the house did not fall very fast.

The pig used guile as fast as he could,
With Miss Riding Hood.

Hood came with a flash,
But Goldilocks came with her whiplash.

They had an enormous fight,
Which killed them both with a fright.

The famous Goldilocks won again,
With her famous anger and pain.

Marc Burnett (10)
Dunn Street Primary School

The New Improved Little Red Riding Hood

Once upon a rhyme from a dark wood
Grandma called Red Riding Hood

The wolf was bothering Grandma
She was in quite a stir

Grandma asked, 'Will you go and get my bread?'
While she was gone the wolf locked her in the shed

The wolf waited for Red Riding Hood
He hid behind the cupboard stood

Red Riding Hood heard Grandma bellow
So did a woodcutter dressed in yellow

The woodcutter offered his advice
But she just slapped him harshly twice

While he ran around and stuttered
She pinched his shiny woodcutter

The wolf was guarding the shed
Red Riding Hood chopped him dead

Grandma was set free
They went and had some tea

Grandma heard what Red Riding Hood had done
It didn't sound as if she'd had much fun

Grandma started howling
Miss Hood was prowling

From her basket she drew a gun
With just one shot Grandma was done!

Andrew Nelson (10)
Dunn Street Primary School

Jack's Back

Jack, that horrible little thief
I'm going to call that police chief

He always gives frights
Starts lots of fights

He picked up a hook
People started to look

One day he started a big fight
With many people who were bright

He started to drive a car
He only went to a bar

He got to a giant's house
He looked like a big mouse

He went to the beach for a drive
Instead he only took a dive

Jack ran through the hall
He kicked the football

Hit the giant's head
Put him in his bed

He went to his mam
She gave him some ham

The giant began to shout
He started a bout

Jack kicked the ball
Sent the giant through the hall.

Connor McGurran (11)
Dunn Street Primary School

Criminal Law!

Once upon a rhyme
Some aunts committed a crime

They locked her in a cellar
Poor! Poor Cinderella!

They all began to shout
'Is Baby Bear about?'

They knew something was wrong
Because she wasn't singing her song

Her belly started to rumble
So people started to tumble

Everyone started to panic
It's just like the Titanic!

When Baby Bear heard about this
'This is something I can't miss!'

He went in the spooky wood
And found clever Miss Riding Hood

They ran as fast as they could
Through the dark and spooky wood

They sprinted through the locked and bolted door!
'Your aunts have broken the criminal law!'

Cinderella jumped and yelped
'Hurry! Hurry! I need some help!'

They demolished Cinderella, poor girl
Riding Hood put on the dress to give us a whirl!

They had a meal on the way
And pinched the dress for a special day!

Baby Bear and Riding Hood wed
Guess in whose beautiful and colourful dress?

Kayleigh Bramwell (11)
Dunn Street Primary School

The Real Story Of Cinderella

Cinderella was so sad,
As her stepmother was so bad!
'Please come help me!' she did cry
'Or one day, I'm sure to die!'
So in her Porsche she did go
She searched the land high and low!
'Who will help me?' she did pray
'Lots of money I will pay!'
Then by chance he appeared
A weird man with a beard!
Then he whispered in her ear
'Listen to me, little dear
You must do this and do that
Then gone will be that fat rat!'
She responded, 'Thank you very much!'
And left that clever man in a rush
Tragic was her life
Why did Daddy take a wife?
So her dad she tried to force
To go to court for a divorce!
'You may lose the big old house
But on your money she can't pounce!'
He signed his name on the form!
Cinderella felt ever so warm!
Soon her plan was working well
The ogre can go to Hell!
She was happy, she was glad
No more her life would be sad!
So just as she begun
Cinderella, she had won!

Victoria Temple (11)
Dunn Street Primary School

Winter

Winter has come with all the cold snow,
Winter has brought a sleigh out of the house,
Winter has found our hats, scarves and gloves,
Winter has forced animals to hibernate.

Winter has brought all the slippery ice,
Winter has made us wrap up very well,
Winter has brought Christmas along,
Winter has put black ice on the road,
Winter has paid Jack Frost a lot.

Joe Moore (9)
Dunn Street Primary School

Parents

P leased to see you do well
A nnoying and so bossy
R idiculous and shouty
E xcited and sometimes happy
N eed your help for everything
T hey always show you up
S ome are smart and some are not
because that's parents for you.

Amy Cook (10)
Dunn Street Primary School

Animals

There are cats that purr, there are dogs that bark,
There are rats and bats in the dark.
Leopards and tigers are fast
And a tortoise is so slow, it will come last.
But there are giraffes with very long necks,
And birds like robins and pigeons that peck.
But I guess there isn't enough time to see them all.

Leah Dawson (10)
Dunn Street Primary School

Know Me?

I'm sly and quick,
I love to lick,
Know me? I'm a cat.

I always fly,
I never try,
Know me? I'm a bat.

I jump and go,
Splash and flow,
Know me? I'm a whale.

I slip and slide,
Sometimes glide,
Know me? I'm a snail.

I jump and run,
Having fun,
Know me? I'm a human.

Paula Slator (9)
Dunn Street Primary School

Children

Children are noisy,
Children are happy,
Children are quiet,
Children are messy and some are nice,
Children are big and small,
Children are happy when others are sad,
Some children chat when other ones don't,
Some children eat crisps when other ones don't,
Children play hide-and-seek and tell jokes.

Nicola Temple (10)
Dunn Street Primary School

Animals

My favourite is Australian
It's called a kangaroo
I also like the koala
And those are my favourite too

I like a range of animals
The hamster and the gerbil too
They are also two of my favourites
As well as the kangaroo.

Chantelle Burns (9)
Dunn Street Primary School

Animals

In the world there's lost of different animals
People keep some animals in their house
Like cats and dogs but no hogs or frogs
Animals live in different places
And they se lots of new faces
They live in the zoo and meet kangaroos
Farms are full of different creatures like ducks and horses
Children even draw their pictures.

Sophie Joyce (10)
Dunn Street Primary School

10 Things Found In A Little Boy's Pocket

Two red sweets
A yummy treat
Even snowballs stuck on the walls
A toy gun
A yummy bun
Even a little bug and a big rug
And a sticky toffee and yummy coffee.

Adam Watson (10)
Hetton Primary School

What Is . . . The Wind?

It is a wolf, howling and blowing
through the hills and valleys

It is an angry god running around the
world (and making strong winds)

It is a herd of elephants trumpeting
loudly and heard around the whole world

It is spinning tops in the sky
spinning around and around fiercely.

Adam Camsell (9)
Hetton Primary School

Thunder

Thunder is a big bang
It makes you jump

Thunder sky is black and grey
It makes a loud crash

Like God playing drums
Like clouds crashing together in the sky.

Craig Williams (10)
Hetton Primary School

What Are Clouds?

It's like a large ball of candyfloss,
A huge soft snowball,
A really sweet shot of Heaven,
Showers of sheep shooting through the sky,
A fluffy pillow,
A plump bed lying in mid-air.

Courtney Price (9)
Hetton Primary School

What Are Clouds?

Dark clouds are
Like creepy monsters
Spreading a cloak
Across the sky

White fluffy sheep
Leaping all around
The clouds

White feathery beds
That people can
Lie on all day long.

Jade Thomasson (9)
Hetton Primary School

10 Things Found In A Clown's Pocket

A red nose
Squirty hose
Joke book
Dirty boot
Poo-flavoured sweets
PS2 cheats
Bouncy balls
Juggling snails
A green snot and
A wiggling bot.

Nathan Waters (9)
Hetton Primary School

Stars

Stars are like lamps up in the sky
The moon is like a big flame that stays there for all time
The stars are beautiful in the bright sky like big candles.

Michael James (9)
Hetton Primary School

Excuses, Excuses

Dear Mam,

The cat spilt the jam,
House is full of smoke,
Hoover's broke,
A ghost snapped the mop,
Baby's balloon went pop.

Yours sincerely

Anthony Froud (9)
Hetton Primary School

Absent

Dear Teacher,

I'm sorry for my boy's arrival
But he comes with a rifle
For everyone that comes along
Will soon not belong

My son is full of gore
He'll start the next world war!

Michael Mackel (9)
Hetton Primary School

What Is The Moon?

The moon is a giant silver mirror
reflecting your face

The moon shining like a bright sky
looking at you in the breeze

On the moon it is like floating in Heaven
with all the gods watching above and you looking back.

Lauren Whitehead (9)
Hetton Primary School

Peace

Peace is calm,
It looks like a pure dove,
It sounds like gentle chime bars,
It tastes like warm treacle pudding
And smells like a scented candle,
Peace feels like suede and silk clothing.

Rachel Hancock (9)
Hetton Primary School

Love

Love is nice
It looks like hearts
It sounds like angels singing
It tastes like Heaven
And smells like a gorgeous vanilla candle
Love feels like silk.

Rachael Watson (9)
Hetton Primary School

Love

Love is happy
It looks like flowers
It sounds like angels singing in the sky
It tastes like berries
And smells like fruit
Love feels like peace.

Chelsea Anderson (9)
Hetton Primary School

Happiness Is Love

It looks like Heaven
It sounds like music
It tastes like candyfloss
And smells like flowers
Happiness feels like peace.

Jurate Rozentale (9)
Hetton Primary School

What Is A Storm?

A storm is like a wolf howling at the moon
And like giant's footsteps crashing on cities
Like bombs exploding into flashes of light
And like a mountain crumbling down and shaking the Earth.

Kieran Alderson (9)
Hetton Primary School

Animals And Their Clothes!

My mother is an excellent knitter,
With a drink of something bitter.

Every animal in the garden
Gets some clothes without a 'pardon'!

Birds, rabbits and caterpillars too,
All have woolly jumpers
And bump into car bumpers.

Ants have long boots
And jump a lot of hoops.

Spiders have miniskirts
And owls have smart shirts.

Erin Clydesdale (9)
Highfield Community Primary School

Girls' Clothes!

Girls' clothes are cool
And make boys drool

Socks, socks
Ugly frocks
Make boys want to chuck rocks

Skirts, skirts
Fantastic shoes
You'll see them on the evening news

Boots, boots
Fashion tops
Don't we look top of the pops

Girls' clothes are cool
And make boys drool.

Clare Orrick (10)
Highfield Community Primary School

Clothes And Me

Clothes and me
I always wear my T-shirt
And try and make the guys flirt
I also slip on my skirt
And try my hardest to keep out of the dirt

I once put on my fluffy dress
And then decided, what a mess
I went to see my friend called Tess
And she had something to confess.

Jade Mordue (10)
Highfield Community Primary School

Animals And Their Clothes

Hats, scarves, gloves and so
They all go well on animals
Snails with socks, cats with frocks
They all go well on animals

Birds with gloves, cats with hoods
They all go well on animals

And when there's blizzards, snow and ice
Jumpers, scarves, knitting and stuff
But for some animals it's just tough
They didn't have clothes to keep them warm
But for the rest, they all go well on animals!

Sarah Cairns (9)
Highfield Community Primary School

Tutu

Behold the hippo, shy and sweet
Satin slippers on her feet
Twirling to a drumbeat

Does her tutu seem too small?
Does she sometimes trip at all?
Does her headdress slip at all?

Does it matter where she goes?
Hopeful as a morning rose,
Spinning on her happy toes.

Chloe Logan (9)
Highfield Community Primary School

Clothes And Me!

Clothes, clothes everywhere
Walking around so you can stare
I wear cool trainers
In the rain

Clothes, clothes everywhere
Walking around so you can stare
I have a jumper
Makes me look like an Oompah loompa

Clothes, clothes everywhere
Walking around so you can stare
I have a shirt
I don't have a skirt.

Cameron Simmonds (9)
Highfield Community Primary School

Clothes And Me!

I wear clothes all around the town
I wear clothes till the sun goes down
Purple clothes, red clothes, pink clothes too
Whatever clothes, it's up to you
People think that I am posh
Just because I'm loaded with dosh
Clothes and me, clothes and me
I love clothes and that's just me!

Corie Graham Pritchard (10)
Highfield Community Primary School

Clothes And Me!

Clothes, clothes are so cool,
If you don't like them, you're a fool!
Clothes and me are like butter and bread,
Clothes are so cool when they're red,
I dread,
I fed them all,
I hate jumpers that look like Oompah loompas.

Jack Hall (9)
Highfield Community Primary School

Pets Aren't Good Enough

I went to the pet shop
To buy myself a pet

My mum asked me what I would like
I said a giraffe but he was too necky!

I said a monkey but his bottom was blue!

I said a hyena but he was too laughy!

I said a parrot but he only said 'You!'

I said a rabbit but she was too eary!

I said an elephant but he was too trunky!

I said an aardvark but he was too nosy!

I said a rhinoceros but he was too bulky!

I said a puppy, there was nothing wrong with him,
He was great, I kept him!

Julia Henzell (9)
La Sagesse Junior School

The Angel And I

What is the angel's name?
What is mine?

What is the angel's age?
Mine is nine

Is the angel very bright
In her sparkly dress of white?

Does the angel play the harp
Or am I dark?

Does the angel smile
At least for a while?

Where do you hide your secrets?
Maybe in a file.

Sofia Del Rio (9)
La Sagesse Junior School

My Devil Sister

My devil sister is the devil of the Earth,
But when my sister meets the sun she turns into dirt
My devil sister loves the night,
But hates the sight of daylight.

I wish my devil sister would just disappear,
But when it's the end of every year
She's always very near,
When it's cold, I really like her,
My evil, despicable, devil sister.

Aimee Irwin (9)
La Sagesse Junior School

My Little Bird

Birds tweet with their feathers all soft,
Some live in a nest, some live in the loft.
They sing all night, they sing all day,
They sing in the blossom trees of May.
They fly around and hop, hop, hop,
They swoop right down without having to stop
And then at night she goes to sleep,
There is not a noise, there is not a peep.
Then my bird flies south for the year,
What a tweet and a chatter in her feathery fur!

Ciara McFaul (9)
La Sagesse Junior School

Nonsense Pets

I wish I had an elephant
As big as big can be
I wish I had a rhinoceros
But he would frighten me
I wish I had a kitten
But he would scratch my nose
I wish I had a puppy
Yes, that's the pet I want I suppose.

Katherine Garner (8)
La Sagesse Junior School

My Pony

I have a little pony, his name is Treacle Tart
He's cute and soft and cuddly, he really takes you far
He is lovely to ride and he has no fear
He is as sweet as rose petals and really quite dear
When we are together we really set a trend
My pony really is my very best friend.

Jessica Bamigbade (8)
La Sagesse Junior School

Sisters

Sisters are big pains
They are also very boring
They always sneak up on you
And tell you exactly what to do

My sister is just like that
She tells on me or tells me off
But without my horrible sister here
Boredom is very near.

Caroline Hudson (8)
La Sagesse Junior School

My Sister

I have a sister, she is nice
Sometimes we have a fight
But usually she is always kind
We play games every day
Even though we have a fight
I need my sister all the time
I'm glad I have my sister
I really, really am!

Sarah Gourley (8)
La Sagesse Junior School

Crazy Animal

I had a crazy pet that jumped on me
It wiggled its tail and giggled with glee
I went to the city and I saw a little dog
Standing all alone chewing on a log.

Emily Morton (9)
La Sagesse Junior School

My Mum's Car

My mum's car
Drives so far
We go to the park
But not when it's dark

My mum's car
Shines like a star
My mum cleans
Until it gleams.

Jessica Davidson (8)
La Sagesse Junior School

A Wedding

I once went to a wedding,
It was really good,
She walked down the aisle,
As she knew she should,
She smiled at me
And I smiled at her
And now I am happy,
On the best day of the year.

Emma Briggs (8)
La Sagesse Junior School

My Teddy Bear

My teddy bear is cute and cuddly,
He has a cute face and a nice bow,
He is cuddly but if you put him to face you,
His left arm is as soft as a fluffy cloud.

Lara Allen (8)
La Sagesse Junior School

My Monster Dog

My dog is a little monster
Because late at night he creeps into my bedroom
And pushes my bed and snuggles in for the night

Although he wakes me up at night
I still love him although he is a little monster dog

My dog is a little sneaky, cheeky monkey
He sneakily, creepily stays beside me all night long.

Zena Al-Ani-Taplin (8)
La Sagesse Junior School

My Mum

My mum is the best
She tidies my room
And does my washing
And cleans the playroom
We sometimes watch TV
Just my mum and me
I love my mum more than words can say
And that will stay the same.

Charlotte Louise Dobson (8)
La Sagesse Junior School

My Big Brother

My brother is a pain,
He really, really is,
Sometimes he is,
Sometimes he isn't,
He cannot talk as well as me,
Even though he's ten.

Sophie Phillips (7)
La Sagesse Junior School

Scary, Haunted House

S ending through you jolts of fear
C an you hear
A ghostly wail?
R aking on the wood are claws, like the scratching of a nail.
Y ou feel scared too.

H appiness abandoning you
A nd out comes a vampire,
U nderneath you, a sharp spire.
N ever-ending trails of blood,
T ake to mingling with mud,
E very person there doesn't want to return,
D anger is at every turn.

H ow long can you stand
O minous death in a ghostly land?
U p above you terrible creatures hide,
S taying on the Devil's side,
E veryone is afraid of the haunted house!

Matthew Ridley (10)
Newlands School

Big Dipper

Lingering at the top, ready to go
Adrenalin pumping, heart rate rising
Clinking and clanking of chains
Heart still thumping
Then start moving, slowly gathering speed
Then jerk back and *bang!*
Up, up and up, climbing, climbing
Whoooosh!
Down faster than you've ever been before
Stomach comes up to your mouth
Loop-the-loop, blood rushing to your head
Finally at the stop, off you get and say
'Never again!'

Andrew James Minto (11)
Newlands School

My Poem About Coketown

(From 'Hard Times' by Charles Dickens)

The continuous piercing scream
Of the steam engine,
Rattling through the town.
Serpentine smoke
Wrapping round its prey,
Turning everything into darkness.
The release of the machines
Causing destruction on the people,
Unleashing an ear-splitting sound.
The sewage in the polluted, purple river
Hosted by rats,
Never turning back to its old self.
The dark, dreary black canal
Going on forever and ever,
Stopping to darken people's souls.
Same days, same nights
In the spinning top of life,
Darkness always wins in Coketown!

Peter Smith (11)
Newlands School

Coketown

(From 'Hard Times' by Charles Dickens)

Through the soot and ash,
Lies the unnatural red and black, Coketown.
A river runs like a purple snake,
Reeking like a cess pit.
Stinking canal,
Runs black with sewage,
All light is absorbed into the murky depths.
Huge towers seem to turn into smoke and disappear.
The steam engines move pumping out soot and ash.
Vast piles of buildings, constantly moving machines.
Life in Coketown goes on and on and on,
Just the same as it has been, is and will be.

Neil Pearston (10)
Newlands School

Lord Of The Rings

L egolas has a bow and two daggers.
O rcs with swords ravage across the land.
R adagast the Brown wonders in the woods.
D enethor is dead, so the king will return.

O ff to the black gate they go to give Frodo time to destroy the ring.
F rodo is the ring bearer who is going to the mountain of fire.

T héoden is the king of Rohan and dies in the third one.
H aldir is an elf who will lead the elves into war.
E lrond is the king of Rivendell who fought in the battle
of Middle-earth.

R ivendell is the house of Elrond.
I sildur is the one who cut the ring off Sauron's fingers.
N asty Gollum tries to kill Frodo.
G imli has an axe which is heavy and deadly.
S am will follow Frodo to the end.

James Twaddle (10)
Newlands School

Haunted House

H for the great loud howl of a wolf
A for the ghostly apparition flying over you
U for the UFO flying over the intruders
N for the nightmares that make you quiver
T for the tarantula that makes your heart vanish
E for the eerie echo that makes you petrified
D for the Dracula which sucks your blood out of your body

H for the great horrible sound that is loud
O for the owl which makes you scared
U for the alien UFO that takes you for supper
S for the great screeches of chewed rats
E for the horrible echoes of the ghosts scaring people.

Christopher Summersall (11)
Newlands School

Coketown

(From 'Hard Times' by Charles Dickens)

Through the blackened soot of the skyline
You find the twisted town of Coketown
It was a town of red and black brick
With tall chimneys belching out smoke
Then we come to the steam engines constantly stamping
Up and down
Moving the machinery
The poisoned river so purple with pollution
Leaving a foul smell of discarded waste
Beggars on the street asking for money
With vermin beside them
All people the same, every day the same and even life the same
Life like a spinning top - same all the time
Seconds ticking away of the life of Coketown.

Sam Beaumont-Perkins (10)
Newlands School

Coketown

(From 'Hard Times' by Charles Dickens)

Coketown with the chimneys popping out
With smoke covering the gloomy clouds making
a grey horrible sky, like it is going to pour down with rain.
The steam engines going along
Chattering as they go by and will never stop.
The machines pumping up and down
Like keeping their knees up.
The windows shattering and everything
Falling down like an earthquake.
The streets are covered with rubbish like
Rats chewing on your feet and you cannot walk anywhere.
The horrible ill-smelling purple river bubbling like a dirty bath.
No one will know what will happen
To the disgrace of Coketown.

Christopher Dry (11)
Newlands School

Coketown

(From 'Hard Times' by Charles Dickens)

Look up from the river, on your right faintly you can see Coketown.
A filthy, dark, stinking place.
The chimneys puffing out infernal smoke trails,
as if a snake was shedding its skin or a snail's slime trailing along.
Some buildings made of brick once red but not now,
just about black in filth of smoke from the chimneys and workhouses.
Machinery is rattling the factories like a stampede of angry cattle,
constantly charging the sound coming through the black, dirty town,
giving everyone migraines and killing out their hearing sense.
Steam engines hissed down at the speed of light,
as fast as lighting falling in a storm, or Thor the thunder's hammer.
The smells of discarded waste,
catching the throats of people,
making them choke and gasp for breath.
The town is like a plate being eaten by a giant and going
out of extinction.

Guy Middleton (10)
Newlands School

The Haunted House

In the haunted house of fear
you always think the undead are near

Whenever you hear a little crack
you instantly think there's going to be an attack

Icy air gives you a chill
bats above wait for the kill

Sounds boom out from every gap
while skeleton fingers go tap, tap, tap.

Tom Hudson (11)
Newlands School

Haunted ABC

A for a dead Anglo-Saxon that howls in your face
B for a black bat that tries to bite you al over the place
C for a cannibal trying to get at your face
D for a Dracula whose footprints leave no trace
E for an echoing cry
F for a fiendish Frankenstein that makes your mouth go dry
G for a ghost that howls and yells
H for a horrible hag that shrieks like hell
I for insects that come out at night
J for the jangling chains that wrap around you tight
K for the killer beast ready to kill
L for the laughing hyena making your blood chill
M for the monster that gives you a scare
N for the nit creeping through your hair
O for the owl - king of the night
P for the undead person meant to give you a fright
Q for the quagmires that quiver and quake
R for the robber fly that makes you shake
S for the skeleton who wants to kill
T for a tarantula killing gives him a thrill
U for the UFO that zooms through space
V for the vampire that drinks blood from your face
W for the werewolf that howls as it roams
X for the x-ray of a dead man's bones
Y for the yeti that bites off your head
Z for the zombie that tries to leave you dead.

Anton Minty (10)
Newlands School

Horror ABC

A for an axe that chops away
B for a bat that floats astray
C for a chainsaw that roars of rust
D for the dead withering into dust
E for an exorcist that uses spells and a charm
F for the deadly face of alarm
G for the dying girl that gives a scream and a yell
H for an evil person going to Hell
I for the invisible hand coming from behind
J for the jinx of a sorcerer's mind
K for the knife stabbing out a cry
L for the life about to die
M for a massacre that nobody can defend
N for a nightmare never seeming to end
O for an owl that hoots in the dark
P for phantom making his mark
Q for the quiver of a juvenile
R for the drained rat that smells so vile
S for the spirit that creeps and chills
T for a tarantula that poisons and kills
U for the unusual creak of the floor
V for a vampire that creeps through the door
W for a werewolf that howls in the night
X for the x-ray of a skeleton's fright
Y for a moan and a lingering yawn
Z for a zombie going to his grave at dawn.

Tommy Greene (11)
Newlands School

Coketown

(From 'Hard Times' by Charles Dickens)

Through the blowing smoke and soot,
Coketown crashes away with steam engines whistling.
With big machines vibrating with windows
Like a stampede of buffalo being chased by a cheetah.
The smell of the polluted brown river
Sweeping through the air.
Beggars crying for money.
The farm animals half dead.
The cry of the sick people.
The dirty canal blowing down the polluted river.
People all the same.
Time ticking away.
Years passing like a spinning top.
But this is Coketown.

Edward Forster (10)
Newlands School

Coketown

(From 'Hard Times' by Charles Dickens)

Red bricks piled high
like a towering inferno.
The smoke is rising like a tornado.
Ash covers this dull town
like dirty snow falling, falling from smoky skies.
In every corner of this sad town there is suffering.
The canal is like a black river of ink.
Engines work like there is no tomorrow.
Bang! Bang! Bang!
The repetitive life of these poor souls.
No hope to an end
till they are buried in their holes.

Tom Carr (10)
Newlands School

Coketown

(From 'Hard Times' by Charles Dickens)

In this dreary time, is the dreary life of Coketown
Chimneys loom over the polluted and ill-smelling town
With smoke puffing out every minute, every hour
Machinery rattling windows
Like a savage beast in anger
The high-pitched sound finding people's ears
The river wriggles around the town
Like a lost worm
The reeking smell filling the city
The steam engine's piston repetitively going up and down
Like watching the hands of a clock
Vermin scuttle around the street letting off an acrid smell
Which lingers up people's nostrils
That is what Coketown sounds like *now . . .*

Matthew Deakin (11)
Newlands School

Coketown

(From 'Hard Times' by Charles Dickens)

Through the thick black smoke
was a town of red and black buildings
it had death printed across the town.
There were paupers grabbing at your clothes
some dead, some alive.
Chimneys puffed out trails of smoke like a slithering serpent.
Steam engines rattled windows like a herd of angry rhinos.
The river that ran purple with ill-smelling piles of waste;
a canal like a river of soot.
Round and round the merry-go-round of Coketown
slowly ticking away.

Matthew Thompson (10)
Newlands School

Ghost Train

G for the ghost hooting in the twilight night
H for the haunted knight that gives you a fright
O for the owl hooting as it flies
S for the spooky, eerie cries
T for the train building up speed

T for the tarantula who wants its feed
R for the raven fluttering in the trees
A for the apparition with its clinking keys
I for the invisible man as cold as ice
N for this nightmare - it did me entice.

Thomas Sinclair (10)
Newlands School

England's Acrostic!

E veryone's happy (mostly).
N ow the first country in the world to win at both rugby and football.
G ood schools.
L eader's a nutter
A nd so is parliament.
N ew visitors are welcome.
D ead rich.

Thomas Fraser (11)
Newlands School

Manchester

M agical at footy.
A nyone can play.
N aughty at fouls.
C hester is the worst.
H ome is the best.
E very person watches.
S aturday's match was the best.
T errible at goalkeeping.
E very person watches.
R ough at tackles.

Ubaydullah Iqbal (10)
Newlands School

The Ghost Train

This is the thriller killer ghost train
The chill, the kill, the thrill
You zoom through the tunnel of doom
The zombies will lead you to their lair
With red eyes and tatty ties
They will kill you - why?
It is like a nightmare
To kill the air
To clash your enjoyment of the fair.

Max Graziani (10)
Newlands School

The Pied Piper

The rats invaded Hamelin and all through the street
They were scampering around with their tiny feet
The people had had enough of this; they went to see the mayor
With angry faces and banners held high, it gave him quite a scare

The mayor and the councillor sat in court, their brains were like rock
Then on the door they heard a soft and gentle knock
'Come in,' said the mayor
And in like a viper entered a man by the name of Pied Piper

'I can rid your town of your plague of rats, I've done it all before
In return I ask for 1000 guilders, I don't want anymore'

Into the street the piper went and on his red pipe he started to play
Out came the rats of Hamelin; they would not stop dancing all day
The piper led the rats down to the town river
The rats jumped in one by one and the piper's smile grew bigger

The church bells rang until the steeple rocked
And the piper skipped back to town
But when he asked for his 1000 guilders
He was answered with a frown

'When you asked for your 1000 guilders I told a little lie
You can have 50 instead; with that there is a lot you can buy'

The piper turned on his heel and walked into the street
Now he played a different tune; all of the children were at his feet:

The piper led them up to Koppleberg
The mountain stood tall and proud
Then a door opened in the side
And they walked in without a sound.

Joe Hockings (9)
St Aloysius RC Junior School, Hebburn

Without . . .

Without umbrellas we'd get wet,
Without Baird there'd be no television yet.
Without shoes our feet would be dirty,
Without vacuum cleaners our homes would be dusty.
Without clocks we wouldn't know the time,
Without drama there'd be no pantomime.
Without food we'd all die,
Without gravity we'd all fly.
Without calendars we'd not know the date,
Without fortune tellers we'd not know our fate.
Without our names we'd get mixed up,
Without china we'd not have cups.
Without cars we couldn't get around,
Without our voices there'd be no sound.
Without ships we couldn't go on cruises,
Without Sundays Grandad'd have no snoozes.
Without colour the world would be dull,
Without forces there'd be no push or pull.
Without my mum there'd be no care,
Even though I drive her spare.
Without wood there wouldn't be tables,
Without Aesop there'd not be fables.
Without our eyes we couldn't see,
Without seeds there'd not be trees.
Without the sun there'd be no light,
Without our hands we couldn't hold on tight.
Without reservoirs there'd be no water to drink,
Without soap we'd all stink.
Without lips we couldn't kiss,
Without God there'd be none of this!

Sarah Chinnery (9)
St Gregory's RC JMI Primary School, South Shields

The Seasons

In spring buds grow,
In spring rivers flow,
Flowing down the windy river,
At the start of spring you might shiver,
In spring the little bird hatches,
On the grass there are lots of patches.

In summer the sun shines,
In summer grow lots of limes,
One by one they fall on the ground
And that's where they may be found,
In summer days are longer,
In summer trees are stronger.

In autumn leaves fall off trees,
In autumn there is a slight breeze,
As the leaves make their way to lie on the grass,
Crunch, crunch, they whisper to those who pass,
In autumn trees get bare,
In autumn things sleep just waiting there.

In winter snow does fall,
In winter you cannot play ball,
All the lakes turn into ice,
I really think it is quite nice,
In winter all the leaves rot,
I really like this season a lot.

Catherine Chinnery (7)
St Gregory's RC JMI Primary School, South Shields

My Day At The Zoo

It was early in the morning
I was about to rise
I went down to breakfast
And got a big surprise

'It's tickets to the zoo,' I shouted
'Is Grandma going too?'

We set off quite early
Didn't want to get there late
There were already lots of people
Queuing at the gates

We went to see the polar bears first
Then the penguins and kangaroo
I'm having such a lovely time
I hope that you are too

The bears growled, the lions roared,
At the zoo you could never get bored

Mum said, 'It's time to go now,
It's getting very late'
My day out at the zoo
Was really, really great

Grandma said she had a great day too
But the funniest thing she saw at the zoo
Were the monkeys
They looked just like *you!*

Danielle Thornton (8)
St Gregory's RC JMI Primary School, South Shields

To Welcome My Brother To The World

Someday,
He'll be a famous footballer,
Or a great English teacher,
He'll settle down,
Marry, have a few kids,
Maybe he won't . . .

Someday,
He'll change the world as we know it,
Or maybe he'll travel,
Send postcards from China
Or phone me from Rome.

Someday,
He'll be a big
Strong man,
But I'll always remember
The first time I held him in my arms.

Someday,
He'll have his own hopes and dreams,
Not know that once upon a quiet time,
I closed my eyes and made a wish,
To one day have in my life.

Emily Sleightholme (9)
St Gregory's RC JMI Primary School, South Shields

The Slob

I know a slob, who lives on the couch,
He is more stupid that a bag of sprouts.
He lives on burgers, pizzas and chips,
Now and again a packet of crisps.
His waistline's expanding by the minute,
When it comes to food there is no limit.
His mouth is full of stains off cheesy puffs,
When you tell him to stop, he goes in a huff.
He's just turned eighteen, so beer's a choice,
When he's drunk he's got a karaoke voice.
He wakes all the house when coming from the pub,
He goes in the kitchen then eats all the grub.
He treats his bedroom like a hotel,
You can't go near it because of the smell.
There are rotten socks all over the floor,
You have to tread carefully when opening the door.
He sleeps in a heap,
On old dirty sheets,
He really disgusts everyone he meets.
He flicks through the channels when the day's dawning,
Waiting for his favourite programme, This Morning.
I think slobs are a disgrace
And in my opinion, a waste of space.

Jake Trelease (9)
St Gregory's RC JMI Primary School, South Shields

Megan, My Favourite Horse

There once was a horse called Megan
And I loved her so,
She was a very beautiful browny-black
And loved to trot in the snow.

I loved to ride on her back,
But I only rode on her twice,
It was a fast half an hour,
But I had the time of my life.

I loved to see her friendly face,
I think she liked to see me,
She had beautiful black beady eyes
That she used to stare at me.

The two weeks that I saw her
She waited a while for me,
I saw her cute little smile,
It was very easy to see.

I recognise her in every way,
Especially by her browny-black fur,
She used to stand there like nobody cared,
But she should know that I'll always love her!

Rebecca Doneghan (9)
St Gregory's RC JMI Primary School, South Shields

Bakewell Tart

A lovely bakewell tart,
Sitting on the kitchen bench,
Staring at me with one eye.

The silver wrapper shining
In the morning sun,
The closer I get the more hungry I get.

The fat chubby cherry,
Sitting on the top,
The thick white icing
Shining like the snow.

I needed to eat it,
But I could not,
What if I get caught?

No! No! I thought,
But in one gobble it was gone,
I needed more!
But the box was empty.

'Mam! Where did you say that
Last bakewell tart was?' asked my sister.

Oh no!

Danny Fenwick (8)
St Gregory's RC JMI Primary School, South Shields

The Circus

The circus is one of my favourite things,
Seeing the acrobats on the big high swings.
The silly clowns stand upside-down
And gallop like hooligans all around.

They throw huge, sticky custard pies,
Which go whizzing through the air like flies.
It splats as it hits someone's face
And the custard goes all over the place.

The audience clap and cheer 'Hooray!'
The ringmaster tuts to show his dismay.
He points his finger at the crazy clown
And the clown's goofy smile turns upside-down.

The audience shout out, 'Boo' and 'Hiss!'
But the grumpy old ringmaster won't have this.
He pulls out his water guns to give the crowd a soak,
Then, he laughs - it was only a joke!

Ellen Smith (9)
St Gregory's RC JMI Primary School, South Shields

My Poem

The ground beside me,
As white as snow,
Tottering around is the brownest doe.
I will follow it around wherever she may go,
She lifts up her front legs, then hangs them down low.

On the grass beside me,
Stands a prowling lion,
He looks like my brother, Ryan.
Like the time he thumped himself and then started crying,
Mum blamed me, but now we all know that he was lying.

There in front of me,
Is a very spotty cheetah,
My sister, Rita
Says that I am neater
At writing her new language 'feel te leater'.

Laura Crutwell (8)
St Gregory's RC JMI Primary School, South Shields

Chocolates

Chocolates are brown,
Chocolates are white,
Chocolates taste delicious as they are a delight.

Chocolates look wonderful,
Chocolates smell delicious,
Chocolates are like winning the lottery!

In the firing hot sun,
Hard chocolates melt,
Making it soft, warm and scrumptious.

I love chocolates,
So should you,
Chocolates taste so lovely,
Chocolates smell so good,
I just have to say that chocolates are fantastic!

I do not know why chocolates were made,
I am so glad they were,
I just wonder is there anymore chocolate?

When I go to the shop, it is so hard to choose,
There's so many chocolates I want,
I get so excited,
My tummy does as well!

Jack Allen (8)
St Gregory's RC JMI Primary School, South Shields

Space Adventures

Whizzing past the asteroids,
Past the Earth and moon,
Now we're heading for the sun,
We better turn back soon.

We're flying in space.

Drinking in the Milky Way,
Chasing all the stars,
Looking up and everywhere,
See Jupiter and Mars.

We're flying in space.

There are all the aliens,
Some look like a jelly,
One has really puffy cheeks,
To match his chubby belly.

We're flying in space.

Safely in our great big rocket,
We are heading home,
We've seen cities on the planets,
There's even one called Comb.

We're flying in space.

Zofia Bungay (8)
St Gregory's RC JMI Primary School, South Shields

Animals

Monkeys can be little tinkers,
Monkeys can be little stinkers,
Monkeys can be very cheeky,
Monkeys can be very freaky.

Guinea pigs are small and cute,
Guinea pigs can't play the flute,
Guinea pigs are soft and furry,
Guinea pigs aren't very scary.

Dolphins are grey and white,
Dolphins have excellent eyesight,
Dolphins are great swimmers,
Dolphins aren't very good singers.

Owls are very wise,
Owls don't eat flies,
Owls fly out in the dark,
As quiet as a skylark.

Dogs can be big or small,
Dogs can be very tall,
Dogs can be really loud,
Dogs can look extremely proud.

Rabbits are so loveable,
Rabbits are really huggable,
Rabbits are really cute,
Rabbits aren't minute.

Amy Allen (9)
St Gregory's RC JMI Primary School, South Shields

A Ghost's Story

Through my mind I wander
In the shadows of your love
My love for you shone like a torch
Like a turtle dove

My life it changed forever
My heart and soul stood still
Knowing we were together
In my spine I felt a chill

I hoped it would last forever
'Till death us do part'
I knew it would definitely happen
You had stolen my heart

But on that dreaded day
For the army I was called
I had to leave you, there was no choice
I remember all day I bawled

For years I sniped in that cold, damp trench
Aiming for their head
But the enemy stormed our trenches
And I quickly shot dead

Thus ends my tale of sadness
Though my love for you will remain
I shall never forget you
Now I cannot feel even the rain.

Paul McStea (11)
St Gregory's RC JMI Primary School, South Shields

Holiday Of A Lifetime

We went on holiday
It was dead sunny
My family were there
It was really quite funny

When we went snorkelling
Under the sea
My big brother
Was far more scared than me

We went to the shops
And saw Britney Spears
My dad was amazed
So he drank lots of beers

We went to the beach
And lazed by the sea
My big brother took his girlfriend
On a jet ski

Outside our room
Was a pool full of turtles
They swam and they swam
But only in circles

We went to the pool
To watch sharks being fed
Bull sharks, reef sharks
And even a hammerhead

When it was time to go home
I wanted to stay
Our flight was delayed
Hip hip hooray.

Callie Foreman (9)
St Gregory's RC JMI Primary School, South Shields

Seasons!

The morning sun begins to rise
My eyes open beneath the new sky
The colours brighten up the night
And a glorious day meets my sight
I hear birds beginning to whistle and sing
I see flowers appear, for it is spring!

As time moves on, it turns to summer!
The best of all seasons and to explain I'll give you some reasons
I like to swim in the pool, as it's so hot it makes me cool
But the best thing of all is there's no boring school!
I laugh and play with my friends
I hope these days will never end
But as you know summer doesn't last
Better run to enjoy it fast
For all too soon the wind will blow
And autumn leaves begin to show

Shorts and T-shirts change to coats
Days start to shorten as it grows cold
A blanket of leaves cover the grass where I played
Return to school as always
Flowers and birds start to disappear
As the weather changes winter draws near

As temperatures drop low, from the sky falls snow
The cold white flakes make my cheeks glow
Snowballs and sledging is what I like best
Building a snowman is always a test
Christmas brings joy from the cold outside
Parties and presents in this happy Yuletide
Winter seems to last forever
But soon it will change for the better!

Megan Gibson (11)
St Gregory's RC JMI Primary School, South Shields

Some Fun In Winter

It's wonderful when winter comes
And snow falls on the ground,
As this is the time that I love best
And I wish it was all year round.

My friends and I find lots to do,
On ice we all go sliding,
As we shout and laugh and have fun,
We feel like we are gliding.

I like building a snowman in my garden,
Which is always really good fun,
But later on when the temperature rises,
I find he has melted in the sun.

We all bring out our sledges,
For sliding down the hills,
But hope we don't hit any rocks,
As that really kills.

I know when it is time to go home,
When my hands and feet are cold,
But I will soon be playing out again,
As I am really bold.

Philip Gray (10)
St Gregory's RC JMI Primary School, South Shields

An Ode To My Dear Friend

My dear friend,
You've been with me all my life,
A helping hand you'll always lend,
I hope that you'll stay with me for evermore;
From the start, to the end.

You help me through the harsh times,
My love you'll never reduce,
You've helped clean up my accidents
And you've mopped up my spilt juice.

You gave me my birthday,
You gave me my life,
You've stood with me through my pain,
And helped me through my strife.

I can always be happy,
As it all fits into place,
All those memories and questions
Every time I see your face.

I can always remember
A broken heart you can always mend,
I hope you can always support me,
My dearest of dear friends.

Lauren Hall (10)
St Gregory's RC JMI Primary School, South Shields

Down By Waterfall Lake

Down by Waterfall Lake,
A snowy-white unicorn stands,
Watching her graceful reflection
And surrounded by emerald lands.

Down in the sapphire, turquoise sea,
A mermaid's amber scales flicker in the light,
As she gently swims with glee.

Up in the starry night sky,
The Pegasus' golden hooves glitter in the moonlight,
The cloudy wing gave permission to fly.

The ruby wings with a glint of gold of a phoenix,
Was born from the blood of a Greek goddess,
A friend of Venus.

On the other side of the world in the sandy deserts,
A sphinx with its wings of a bird,
The head of a human,
But this creature cannot be heard.

Deep in the dark soggy mountain,
A wise trusty dragon sleeps
And from his mouth comes a fiery fountain.

Deep in the thick forest,
A beautiful centaur roams,
It is a trustworthy creature and is deeply honest.

Katherine Shutt (11)
St Gregory's RC JMI Primary School, South Shields

Dragon

Dragon beautiful
Dragon mean
Dragon smooth
Dragon lean

Fangs sharp
Fangs shiny
Fangs deadly
Fangs sparkling

Dragon scaly
Dragon tough
Dragon colourful
Dragon rough

Dragon steaming
Dragon hiss
Dragon mythical
Dragon *myth!*

Rebecca Grant (10)
St Gregory's RC JMI Primary School, South Shields

Dogs

Fast runner
Bird hater
Treat lover
Walk liker
Dinner wanter
Cat chaser
Wash unliker
Good player
Bone digger
Funny scratcher
Bad climber
Black and white strayer.

Jackson Beal (7)
St James' RC Primary School, Hebburn

My Brother

Quick-runner
High-jumper
Strong-fighter
Light as a feather
Loud-shouter
Big-brother
Trick-catcher
Bad-climber
Bad-swimmer
Sleek-walker
Light-walker
Wicked-rocker
Wide-brother
Smart-worker
Quick as a robber
Wicked-brother
Trick-teacher.

Stephanie Redford (8)
St James' RC Primary School, Hebburn

A Frog

Swift mover,
Amazing swimmer,
Ear-splitting croaker,
Thrilling leaper,
Skilful climber,
Lily pad glider,
Insect muncher,
Strong licker,
Bug follower,
Clever thinker.

Connor Saul (8)
St James' RC Primary School, Hebburn

Bird!

High flier
Non dier!

Egg hatcher
Worm catcher!

Good swimmer
Likes dinner!

Has a feather
Feels like leather!

Clever thinker
Is a tinker!

Nest maker
Winter hater!

Little soft creature
Has a very big feature!

Winged glider
High rider!

Likes summer
Happy hummer!

Good tweeter
Worm beater!

Josh Hills (7)
St James' RC Primary School, Hebburn

Green Frog

Rapid jumper
Fly catcher
Fine swimmer
Great eater
Lily pad hopper
Loud croaker.

Scot Neilands (8)
St James' RC Primary School, Hebburn

Snake

Slimy slider
Tree climber
Super disguiser
Sneaky hider
Poisonous killer
Slow mover
Excellent hisser
Good chomper
Sharp biter
Dangerous eater
Amazing cruncher
Humungous grower
Best swimmer
Wild hunter
Weird habits
Hard strangler
Slimy swallower.

Kieran Roberts (8)
St James' RC Primary School, Hebburn

A Rainbow

A rainbow is a multicoloured slip
Thrown into the sky

A rainbow is a colourful classroom
In a colour land

A rainbow is some colourful pens
Leaking all over the water

A rainbow is disco lights
Shining over the sky.

Aidan Clarke (9)
St James' RC Primary School, Hebburn

Dog

Fast runner
Quick eater
Nice player
Loud barker
Light sleeper
Bone licker
Cute swimmer
Funny crier
Fast leaper
Loud scratcher
Little growler
Late sleeper
Fast drinker
Toy squeaker.

Laura Blake (7)
St James' RC Primary School, Hebburn

Jock The Dog

Furry biter
Cat catcher
Quick mover
Loud barker
Great paddler
Food snatcher
Arm scratcher
Peace shatterer
Nice actor
People teaser
Wild runner.

Rosie Burke (8)
St James' RC Primary School, Hebburn

Young Dolphin

It dazzles through the night
In the sunlight
And makes a sound
You get a nasty shiver
Down your spine
It gleams and stares
Through the sun
Swiftly jumps
Through the air and goes.

Amy Bone (8)
St James' RC Primary School, Hebburn

Mum!

Bottom nipper,
Loud shouter,
Homework checker,
Hug giver,
Cool kisser,
Home time lover,
Rain hater,
Cheeky monster,
Food buyer,
Dinner cooker!

Bethan Hewitt (8)
St James' RC Primary School, Hebburn

The Rainbow Is . . .

The rainbow is stripy socks you wear
The rainbow is a stained glass window
A boomerang whizzing colours in the sky
The rainbow is coloured flowers in a field
A rainbow is a multicoloured beach ball thrown in the sky.

Rachel Stothard (10)
St James' RC Primary School, Hebburn

Rabbit

Best hopper
Mean biter
Fur puller
Cabbage eater
Bad growler
Carrot eater
Tail bobber
Quick runner
Wicked jumper
Nose twitcher
Whisker wiggler.

Lee Walsh (7)
St James' RC Primary School, Hebburn

Emily's Rabbit

Fast runner,
Excellent hopper,
Good hider,
Great digger,
Quick scurrier,
Silent creeper,
Soft sleeper,
Loud squeaker!

Emily Hackett (7)
St James' RC Primary School, Hebburn

A Cloud Is . . .

The colour is like candyfloss in the sky so high
It's a fluffy white feather floating in the sky
I see cotton wool in the sky very high up
It's like a flock of white sheep
And they make me go to sleep.

Jordan Young (9)
St James' RC Primary School, Hebburn

The Moon Is . . .

Like a fluffy, round pillow that is white
Laying on a dark, black, patterned bed
With bright white dots

A big, pale, white balloon filled with helium
Flying right up to the dark sky
Scared in case it hits a star and goes *pop*

An inventor trying to draw something
That he is going to invent and throwing
Paper to the base of the bin getting annoyed

Tinfoil floating in a blue river.

Jamie Carty (10)
St James' RC Primary School, Hebburn

Lucky, The Dog

Loud barker,
Quick runner,
Tail wager,
Ace fetcher,
Big biter,
Ball lover,
Cat chaser,
Bone chewer!

George Currie (8)
St James' RC Primary School, Hebburn

The Moon

The moon is a football kicked high in the sky
The moon is a ten pence piece rolling on a table
The moon is a splodge of glue on a black piece of paper
The moon is a white clock on a black wall.

Ryan Mills (9)
St James' RC Primary School, Hebburn

The Moon, The Rainbow

The moon is . . .
A white giant gobstopper on a plate
A white football kicked into the sky
A splodge of ice cream on a piece of paper
A white fluffy pillow in the sky
A giant white snowball
A crumpled piece of paper
A little white bouncy ball
A top off a water bottle
A rubber.

The rainbow is . . .
A multicoloured flower in a garden
A coloured hat on the floor
A coloured ball in the sky
A splodge of multicoloured ice cream
Spray paint multicoloured.

Nikki Spence (9)
St James' RC Primary School, Hebburn

The Moon Is . . .

The moon is a big splodge of ice cream
The moon is a giant's white gobstopper
The moon is maybe a dream
Wow, the moon is a large whopper
If your hardest is high, why don't you throw it all up in the sky?
The moon shines over at night
The moon has a pretty face
The moon is very bright
I wish you could lock it in a suitcase
If a giant has a big kite
You could fly the kite all the way up to space.

Amy Coyne (9)
St James' RC Primary School, Hebburn

A Cloud Is . . .

A cloud is like a feather pillow on a blue sheet
On a king-sized bed

A cloud is like a cotton ball
On the side of the riverbed

A cloud is like a white sheet floating in the sky
It might be hard, it might be soft or some apple pie

A cloud is like a bowl of mash that was dropped on
The blue carpet or some fruit in the exotic

A cloud is like a scrunched-up piece of paper
Rolling along the table

But I think a cloud is some steam
Or some cotton wool in the sky

But I guess we will never find out.

Raylee Lawrence (10)
St James' RC Primary School, Hebburn

The Stripy Rainbow

The rainbow is a stripy colourful tie
Where a giant lies when it's raining

The rainbow is an arch bridge from cloud to cloud,
That people walk on.

The rainbow is a lollipop that I would like to eat
On my stripy coloured seat.

The rainbow is a coloured pen
That I write with every day.

The rainbow is a coloured wire
Inside my stripy plug.

Adam Crozier (10)
St James' RC Primary School, Hebburn

The Clouds And A Rainbow

A cloud in the sky
A cloud is a big steam train with puffs of smoke
Candyfloss made by a giant
A bag of wool in the sky above
When a big splodge fell in the sky
White hair lying high up in the sky
A big white cloud in the sky
Like a pillowcase in the sky
A bag of marshmallows in the sky

A rainbow in the sky
A coloured cape in the sky
A star in coloured shapes
A coloured balloon in the sky.

Andrew Kidger (9)
St James' RC Primary School, Hebburn

A Rainbow

A rainbow is some sugar candy.
A rainbow is a big bowl of jelly.
A rainbow is a sparkly dress.
A rainbow is a little flower in my garden.
A rainbow is a slide that I go on.
A rainbow is a soft, sweet banana.
A rainbow is like some disco lights.
A rainbow is like some stripy socks.
A rainbow is like a curly wig on my head.
A rainbow is like a pen that is all colours.
A rainbow is a football kicking around.
A rainbow is a wriggly path I walk on.
A rainbow is a skipping rope.

India Radick (10)
St James' RC Primary School, Hebburn

The Moon And A Cloud

The moon is like a big plate in the sky
The moon is a big piece of cheese
The moon is a big milk bottle top
It is a white pea in the sky
It is a blob of milk
A ball of glass in the night sky
An ice cream that jumped into the sky
A football that got kicked into the sky

A cloud is an old man's wig that he threw in the air
And got stuck there
It is a rug that flew into the sky
It is a spray of grey paint on a blue background
It is cotton wool in the sky
It is a ball of candyfloss in the light blue sky.

Sarah Henley (10)
St James' RC Primary School, Hebburn

A Rainbow

A rainbow is like the gate to Heaven
With stained glass windows and a cupful of colours
There could be stripy snakes living up there
There could be a book full of colours
In a rainbow there could be a fair with coloured rides
And a multicoloured roller coaster
Everyone could wear coloured socks in the winter
People could wear a coloured scarf
People might go to the park and children go down a coloured slide
People might wear multicoloured jumpers
And when there's a disco on, there will be coloured disco lights.

Paige O'Neill (9)
St James' RC Primary School, Hebburn

A Cloud Is . . .

A cloud is a very fluffy pillow
Or a snowball tossed
It can even be a marshmallow
Or a stick of candyfloss

It could be a plate of mash
Or something that you pull
Instead of mash it could be smash
Or is a bit of cotton wool

It might be hard, it could be soft
Or something that you cuddle
It might be dry, it might be moist
A cloud is a giant bubble.

Anthony Brennan (9)
St James' RC Primary School, Hebburn

The Rainbow

The rainbow is disco lights shining all around
The rainbow is multicoloured socks lying in your bedroom
The rainbow is a colourful butterfly fluttering in the spring
The rainbow is multicoloured skipping ropes when people
are playing in the playground
The rainbow is colourful stain glass window on the front of
your white door.

Alexandra Crozier (10)
St James' RC Primary School, Hebburn

Clouds

Clouds are bubbles over a nice hot bath
A cloud is a white horse fighting on a blue battlefield
A cloud is a splodge of ice cream on a giant tea plate
A cloud is a white ballerina dancing in the blue spotlight.

Roxanne Saul (9)
St James' RC Primary School, Hebburn

A Cloud, The Moon, A Rainbow

A cloud is a fluffy white jumper,
A cloud is a white shopping bag floating peacefully in the midday sky,
A cloud is gas coming from a power plant's chimney
A cloud is a tattered piece of paper
A cloud is a blob of ice cream on a blue piece of paper

The moon is a ball kicked into the midnight sky
The moon is a scrunched-up ball of paper
The moon is a white golf ball whacked into the sky

A rainbow is a multicoloured banana held up in the sky
A rainbow is a bent cable wire, high in the white sky.

Alex Deacon (10)
St James' RC Primary School, Hebburn

The Moon

The moon is like a football kicked into the sky
It is like a piece of paper scrumpled up and chucked in a blue bin
It is a white balloon floating into the dark blue sky
It is a giant gobstopper in a blue tub
It is a splodge of ice cream on a plate
It is a speedboat speeding on the sea
It is a fluffy pillow on a blue quilt
It is a snowball chucked on a blue coat
It is a circle of tin foil on a blue sheet of paper.

Caitlin Tallack (9)
St James' RC Primary School, Hebburn

The Moon

Everyone says that the moon is cheesy
Though being on it would make me queasy
I wonder what it's like being on the moon
But for now I'll eat cheese with a spoon.

Sean Barron (10)
St James' RC Primary School, Hebburn

The Moon Is . . .

The moon is a snowball thrown into the sky
The moon is a ten pence piece dropped in a drain
The moon is a splodge of glue on black paper
The moon is a white balloon floating in water
The moon is an apple pie with sugar and sweet
The moon is a scoop of ice cream that will hide the horrible wheat
I'll hold the moon in my head
And I'll never ever get out of my bed.

Ayesha Jobes (10)
St James' RC Primary School, Hebburn

A Rainbow

A rainbow is a multicoloured belt on a big belly!
A rainbow is a multicoloured pen in my tray!
A rainbow is a fruity, tasty sweet that I eat!
A rainbow is a multicoloured torch that shines bright at night!
A rainbow is a multicoloured mat on my floor!
A rainbow is a multicoloured wig on my head!
A rainbow is a multicoloured dress that I wear!
A rainbow is a multicoloured snake that slithers around!

Clarece Kew (9)
St James' RC Primary School, Hebburn

Lizard

Fast on water
Slow under
Great climber
Like a spider
Good biter
Excellent runner
It's a sneaker
Insect eater.

Callum Hamilton (7)
St James' RC Primary School, Hebburn

The Moon And A Cloud

The moon is a splodge of ice cream
The moon is a fluffy pillow on a blue bed
The moon is a piece of paper in a blue bin
The moon is a snowball thrown into the sky
The moon is a tea plate thrown into a midnight sky
The moon is a ten pence piece put into a blue money box
The moon is a white football kicked into the midnight sky

A cloud is a big sheet in the sky
A cloud is a big, grey, fluffy mat on a blue carpet
A cloud is a woolly hat on a blue head
A cloud is a big, fluffy dog on its blue shed.

Alex Forshaw (10)
St James' RC Primary School, Hebburn

A Rainbow

A rainbow is like a multicoloured belt in the sky.
It is a multicoloured hair band in a shop.
It is a multicoloured soak on someone's foot.
A rainbow is like a sweet in your mouth.
A rainbow is like a multicoloured gel pen on paper.
It is a multicoloured snake in the jungle.
A rainbow is a multicoloured jumper.
A rainbow is a light at a disco.
It is a multicoloured gate in a garden.
A rainbow is like multicoloured stains on a window.
It is a sweet wrapper from a sweet.

Melissa Crozier (10)
St James' RC Primary School, Hebburn

The Beach

As I walked slowly along the beach,
With the sound of waves and sand at my feet.
I picked up shiny pebbles and washed them in the sea,
While I watched an old couple on the rocks drinking tea.
The breeze was very cool and gentle and shivered up my spine,
I love this time of year, it makes me feel so fine.
Sandcastles, candyfloss and ice cream too
Are all the lovely things you see at the beach.
All children love them, how about you?

Abby Wotherspoon (10)
St Mark's RC Primary School, Westerhope

My Brother

My brother is a waste of time,
He's committed a big crime,
He's stole a shoe from a shop,
He's pulled the hair out my mum's mop,
He's also nipped me with his nails
And has won at heads and tails,
My clothes he has torn,
But the worst crime was being *born!*

Chardonnay Pattison (10)
St Mark's RC Primary School, Westerhope

Animals

A is for aardvarks with a long and pointy snout,
N is for newts wriggling in the pond,
I is for iguanas who sit and laze about,
M is for monkeys swinging high up through the trees,
A is for antelopes bounding over the plain,
L is for lions fearsome, strong and brave,
S is for snakes with a slither, hiss hiss!

Alexandra Parsons (11)
St Mark's RC Primary School, Westerhope

Back In Time

I wish I could go back in time,
To see what happened in the Great War,
I wish I could see how they fought,
To make things different.
I would try to change things that went wrong,
I wish I could go back in time,
To see what life would be like without computer games,
When children made their own games.
I wish I could go back in time,
To meet old and famous people,
To shake hands with them
And ask questions about their lives,
But I know I can't go back in time.

Daniel Connell (11)
St Mark's RC Primary School, Westerhope

Horses

No two are the same,
No two can play a game.

All shapes and sizes,
All kinds of naughty surprises.

Some naughty ones like to go,
Some calm ones really like the word 'Whoa!'

Some take the bits steady and fine,
Others, if they could talk, they'd just whine.

Some buck and kick and they end up fine,
So anytime you need to unwind, your horse is there for you to *ride!*

Jade Lockey (10)
St Mark's RC Primary School, Westerhope

I Love It Here

There I lay
In the middle of the sea
The waves splashing up and down
The wind whizzing through my ear

I love it here
I have no fear
So peaceful, so quiet
I have no interruption

I love it here
I see the birds flying over my head
The noise they make
As they fly over the sea

I love it here
The dolphins that splash in and out
The fishes that wiggle underwater
So peaceful, so quiet.

Rosa Asghari (11)
St Mark's RC Primary School, Westerhope

Football

Football may just be a game,
From free kicks you need a perfect aim.

Running up and down the wing,
The crowd always happy to sing.

Shoot, shoot, the crowd cheers,
Sometimes they turn into tears.

Players will give it their all,
To score that winning goal.

Lee Barnett (11)
St Mark's RC Primary School, Westerhope

Fun, Fun, Fun

Fun, fun, fun
I love fun
Playing board games
And playing with my friends

Fun, fun, fun
Fun is great
Playing on my computer
And playing with my dog

Fun, fun, fun
When I have fun I feel happy
Playing paper games
While sitting in the car

Fun, fun, fun
I have fun with my friends
I have fun with my dog
I have fun in the car
Every day I have *fun!*

Hannah Davidson (11)
St Mark's RC Primary School, Westerhope

The Wind

The cold wind blows through the cemetery,
Rushing around like Tom and Jerry.

The cold wind blows around my mates,
As they try to run through the rattling gate.

The cold wind blows through an abandoned house,
As quiet as the squeak of a tiny mouse.

The cold wind blows on an icy road,
Just as the weatherman had showed.

Holly Davidson (10)
St Mark's RC Primary School, Westerhope

Being An Orphan

Being an orphan is just like not living,
Day after day waiting for the one
Who will take you home and love you like a sibling,
So you will have a family.

Being an orphan is the only bad thing,
You feel so empty and cold inside,
You wait years for the bell to ring
And a mam and dad to take you home.

Being an orphan is like having no heart,
No warming inside you,
You don't dream of being smart,
Just look out the window.

Being an orphan is the worst life to live,
You wake up on Christmas
And all you want is a family to give,
Just stare at the couples.

Being an orphan ruins your life,
You dream of some parents
And hearing the word 'wife',
Then you wake up.

Being an orphan is wanting to run away,
To live on the streets,
Someone could find you and love you, you pray,
So thank the Lord you have a family and never say otherwise!

Kurtis Jones (11)
St Mark's RC Primary School, Westerhope

My House

My house is cosy and warm
With beams on the ceiling and wood on the floor
It's painted and bright and lit up at night
Which all put together
Is a cosy, nice sight.

Luke Pittiglio (10)
St Mark's RC Primary School, Westerhope

Months

January brings celebrations all around
Sleet and snow hits the ground

February brings all the love
Staring at the sunsets up above

March brings rain and hailstones
While digging up dinosaur bones

April brings the Easter bunny
And the bees make lots and lots of honey

May brings pretty daffodils
While you're hiking up all the hills

June brings blossoms on the trees
And loads of flowers full of bees

July brings the hot weather
And all the birds drop a feather

August brings sunny beaches
It also brings the ripe peaches

September brings the end of the summer holidays
And summer has been in every way

October means it's already fright time
Sucking lollies orange, strawberry and lime

November brings Remembrance Day
We buy poppies and help to pay

December brings cold nights
Lots of fun and snowball fights.

Nicole Banks (9)
St Mary's RC Primary School, Newcastle-Upon-Tyne

The Months Poem

January brings cold winter nights
Slush and snow and snowball fights

February brings Mother's Day
And they get presents some way

March brings the cold wet showers
To help grow all the flowers

April brings an Easter bunny
And people call you little honey

May brings the green leaves
Growing on the brown trees

June brings the start of heat
And helps to grow all the wheat

July brings the colourful plants
For a home for all the ants

August brings swirling leaves
Falling down from the trees

September brings Remembrance Day
Where soldiers died far away

October brings Hallowe'en treats
And lots of sweets

November brings the sparkles in the sky
And watch out you don't die

December brings presents today
But you can't get hay!

Brittany McLaren (8)
St Mary's RC Primary School, Newcastle-Upon-Tyne

A Ship

A ship has hulls
And a sail
And some wood.

Wood so strong,
It can face the waves,
Face the anger of the skies.

Can face all weather,
No matter what,
That's a ship!

But what is a ship?
Not hulls or sails or wood -
That's what a ship needs.

But what a ship really is,
That's something different.

Amy Stocker (10)
St Mary's RC Primary School, Newcastle-Upon-Tyne

Dolphins

I think dolphins are rather clever,
Most people have them in their hearts forever.

Dolphins are beautiful and their moves are graceful,
Unlike human beings who can be quite distasteful.

Dolphins can splash
And sometimes clash.

Dolphins are really a special creature,
In the swimming pool they're quite a feature.

Catherine Stothard (9)
St Mary's RC Primary School, Newcastle-Upon-Tyne

A Warning To Eat Properly!

There was a young boy named Reece,
Who was very, very obese.
He sat and watched telly
With ice cream and jelly,
He thought to himself, *what a feast!*

When this young boy went to France,
His mate dragged him up for a dance,
He fell over his mate
Because of his weight,
A poor old boy called Lance!

Reece thought it was such good fun,
But then realised what harm he had done,
'I must go on a diet,
I think I should try it,'
From then on he lived on bread buns!

Reece then became thinner and thinner,
He thought he was onto a winner,
But he didn't look well
And his mum, she did yell,
'I think that you need a good dinner!'

She fed him a nice, healthy meal,
He said, 'How much better I feel!
Don't fill up your belly
With ice cream and jelly,
Include fruit and veg in the deal!'

Rachael Lundgren (10)
St Mary's RC Primary School, Newcastle-Upon-Tyne

The Months

January brings windy breezes
And nasty sneezes!

February brings the cold snow
And the wind starts to blow

March brings the warm spring
And the bees start to come and sting!

April brings stars that shine bright
Children like to go out at night

May brings the baby lambs
Eating by their mams

June brings gloomy caves
And big waves

July brings big flowers
And wet showers

August brings a break
I like to make a cake

September brings the autumn leaves
Gives you a little breeze

October brings the cold
Things start to mould

November brings dull days
My dog stays

December brings Christmas time
Oh no, look at the time!

Lillie Harrison (8)
St Mary's RC Primary School, Newcastle-Upon-Tyne

The Months

January brings snow and sleet
Makes the cold go through your feet

February brings the heavy showers
Then from the ground comes the flowers

March brings the warm breezes
Daffodils and loud sneezes

April brings April showers
Bushes bloom with beautiful flowers

May brings chicks and lambs
Running after their cosy mams

June brings the summertime
And the lovely tangy lime

July brings the sunshine bright
The seas are blue and the sky is light

August brings warm nights
The sunset is a lovely sight

September brings a new class
Summertime has been and past

October brings a cold breeze
Our fingers and toes begin to freeze

November brings Remembrance Day
When we go to church and pray

December brings deep snow
And a frosty cold blow.

Jessica Henderson (8)
St Mary's RC Primary School, Newcastle-Upon-Tyne

Germwocky

(Inspired by 'Jabberwocky' by Lewis Carroll)

'Twas dirty and the mouldy fruit,
Did rot and fester in the bin.
All furry was the nectarine
And the apple-side caved in!

'Beware the disease dogs my son!
The mouth that coughs, the nose that snots!
Beware the dirty cloth and shun
The horrid food that rots!'

He took his soapy sponge in hand,
Long time the fiendish germs he sought,
So rested he with a cup of tea
And stood awhile in thought.

And as in spotless thoughts he stood,
The disease dogs with paws of sham,
Came galloping through the dirt-covered wood
And sneezed as they came!

One, two! One, two! Scrub and clean!
The soapy sponge washed and scrubbed,
He left them clean and feeling keen,
The dogs were then petted and rubbed!

'And hast thou slain the diseased dogs?
Come to my arms, my arms my dirt-free boy!
Oh wondrous day, hip hip *hooray!*'
He shouted in his joy!

Emmie Harrison (10)
St Mary's RC Primary School, Newcastle-Upon-Tyne

Hulksidies

The hulksidies is incredibly strong,
It has a very smelly pong to use for killing,
It has two heads, one for crushing
And one to keep an eye on its victims,
It has a metal head
And by the time someone will find you
You will be dead
Because you have been terminated.

Hulksidies can run a maximum speed of 100 mph,
When it tracks a person down
It gets them until they are dead,
The Hulksidies can be something or someone
So beware, the Hulksidies has come to the future
To kill John Conner because he is going to be the next leader
If the Hulksidies succeeds in killing him
The evil robots will rule the world.

The only person who can kill the Hulksidies
Is the terminator, he is the most mightiest of the machines,
Except for the evil ones,
He will protect the future until the Hulksidies is dead,
Believe the terminator or *die!*

Tahzeela Mohammed (10)
St Paul's CE Primary School, Newcastle-Upon-Tyne

The Amazing Sirens

The sirens are half-bird half-woman,
They are a bit of trouble,
Sing so loud
That you shoot to a cloud.

A sailor went by,
They told a big fat lie
And began to fly.

They cannot be beaten,
Unless they are eaten,
So people thought.

Along came a hero called Ulysses,
Who filled his sailors ears with wax,
Well most of them except Max.

They got beaten
And went to Heaven,
Then never came back again.

Chelsea Francis (9)
St Paul's CE Primary School, Newcastle-Upon-Tyne

Cerberus

Where this great dog lies,
Guarding something secret . . .

The door to the underworld,
Lies right behind him,
All things bad and dead,
Things without a head are here,
Come to this you're dared,
Come to a hungry guard,
Come and be food for the three-headed dog
Cerberus!

Kevin Stobbs (9)
St Paul's CE Primary School, Newcastle-Upon-Tyne

The Gorgons

The gorgons are hideous women with
Serpents instead of hair
They have claws and monstrous teeth
And one glance turns their victims to stone
The gorgons have snakes coming out of their head
The gorgons have a row of teeth
They are not nice creatures
They have big long noses and really sharp teeth
They could bite anyone then turn them into stone easily
If you laugh they will kill you
If you touch them you will get bit by the snakes.

Anne Marie Austin (9)
St Paul's CE Primary School, Newcastle-Upon-Tyne

My Dog

My dog's brown
He's very fluffy
My dad snips his
Coat off in the summer
My dog's the best
Do you think so too?
He sleeps very peacefully
He likes the kitchen better
Than the sitting room
And I do too
A big dog bit him
Bu he bit him back
I love my dog
I would not give him back.

Reece Crake (7)
St Paul's CE Primary School, Sunderland

Larry McRoy

Larry never listens anywhere
And he does not even care
Larry decided to climb a wall
He ended up in the incident hall

It was the big day for the test
In half an hour Larry did his best
There was a little break in-between
And Larry was really keen

The results were announced
And Lisa and Clare bounced and bounced
Larry was feeling very sad
For he had done really bad

Larry did not pass his grade
So he never ever got paid
Clare became a movie star
Lisa worked behind a grubby bar

Larry was in his horrible flat
Stroking his black fat cat
In the room there was a bat
Who ate Larry alive and left the cat

His mother came bursting in to find him dead
Lying across his mucky bed
She said, 'That's my little boy,
The one and only Larry McRoy.'

Beth Gibson (9)
St Paul's CE Primary School, Sunderland

Chris Who Never Shuts Gates

Early one morning
Chris woke up yawning

He went to get ready
Coming down the stairs slow and steady

He goes out and leaves the front door open
He was sitting down on the path and found a token

He goes to the shop and spends it
He had a little sit

Got up and knocked on for his friends
They were at the street's other ends

They went to his dad's barns
And played in the cow's barn

He told them he found a token
Then they went and left the gate open

The cows got out
So did the chickens

When his dad got back to the farm
The chickens and cows had gone

Chickens were flying everywhere
When he got back he got killed by his dad

He went back to the farm and got all of the cows back in the field
Settled all the chickens in the chicken houses

That was his lesson for leaving doors and gates open.

Connor Hutchinson (10)
St Paul's CE Primary School, Sunderland

Tidy Up Billy

Billy's room is such a mess
No one could care about his room any less
It was the messiest in the nation
The only thing he really used was his PlayStation

Along came his friend called Ben
Who kept on blabbing about his new fountain pen
He said, 'Let's go on the top bunk' *crash clank!*
'What have you done, you plank?'

'It wasn't me, it was the toys!'
'What you doing boys?'
Asked Billy's brother, Teddy
'Mam told me to tell you tea is ready'

'Let's go down,' said Billy
'But don't be silly'
Down the stairs to the bottom they went
Teddy was crying, he couldn't get out his tent

But before they both went in for tea
Billy said, 'Don't talk about that boy called Lee'
When they had finished their tea, 'Let's go upstairs,' said Billy
'And we'll watch that show with that woman called Lilly'

Billy ran to his room
But very soon
There was a clash and a clatter
And a smash and a shatter

Poor little Billy was dead

He had fallen and broken his back
On the CD rack
He was a really mucky pup
So always remember to tidy up!

Curtis Smith (9)
St Paul's CE Primary School, Sunderland

The Untidy House

The next day after school had ended
Alex felt quite offended,
For his mum had said, 'Tidy your room
It looks more like a tomb'

He got up and flew out the door
Almost tripping over the floor
Bringing home a friend
Swinging round the stair bend

Walking into his room which looked like a tomb
Stuff bulging out of the doom
All of a sudden a wall did crack
It almost fell onto his back

That day he did tidy his room
Until it didn't look like a tomb
For two weeks later it was back like a tomb
Stuff bulging out of the room

One night the house fell to the ground
And oh what a sound
All because of that one room
Or shall I call it a tomb?

There was one or two legs broken
Nothing was spoken
But you could hear the shouts from miles
For it broke a bathroom tile

Never again was anything untidy
For lying in a hospital
He was not dead
Just his leg red.

Rebecca Hamilton (9)
St Paul's CE Primary School, Sunderland

Colour Poem

Red is for runny blood in my veins
Yellow is for the burning hot sun
Pink is for a snorty pig on the farm
Green is for beautiful grass in the summer
Purple is for lovely juicy grapes
Orange is for a delicious mango
Blue is for yummy blueberries.

Alexandra Meakin (6)
St Paul's CE Primary School, Sunderland

Colour Poem

Red is for big round juicy apples
Yellow is for a big sour lemon
Pink is for soft skin
Green is for green grass in the summer
Purple is for sweet plums
Orange is for tiger stripes
Blue is for cold blue sky.

Katie Renton
St Paul's CE Primary School, Sunderland

Colour Poem

Red is for yummy delicious strawberries
Yellow is for a beautiful daisy
Pink is for a bad tempered pig
Green is for a lovely decorated tree
Purple is for yummy grapes
Orange is for a bad tempered lion
Blue is for a lovely ocean.

Sophie McCluskey
St Paul's CE Primary School, Sunderland

What Is Blue?

I love a blue sky on a summer's day
The stream of water
A flood of oil like a melted sapphire
Blue cars are cool
Paint squiggling from the bottle
Pastel smudging on the paper
Blue water melts the sand round your feet
Blue is everything
Blue is all.

Adam Cowans (8)
St Paul's CE Primary School, Sunderland

Colour Poem

Red is for the fire engine's gleaming paint
Yellow is for the sun's bright light
Pink is for a pig's body
Green is for the grass
Purple is for the delicious grapes
Orange is for the orange juice that we drink
Blue is for the fire engine's flashing lights.

James Atkinson (7)
St Paul's CE Primary School, Sunderland

Fast And Slow

A kitten can run fast
An old cat can't
An old dog can't run fast
A puppy can
A toddler can run fast
An old person can't
I can run fast.

Jordan Foster (7)
St Paul's CE Primary School, Sunderland

What Is Pink?

Pink is a pig that has a curly tail.
Lipstick can be pink,
So can my piggy's tail.
Pink roses are to smell.
Rosy cheeks have no smell.
Pink diamonds are sparkly.
Pink pretty pebble
On a pretty pink table.
A pink hat for winter.
A pink dress for summer.
I would like to be
A pink princess
In a pink castle.

Jordana Loughton (8)
St Paul's CE Primary School, Sunderland

What Is White?

I like white paint
It's soft and white
White paint is the
Best out of the lot
Snow is crunchy
Snow is white
Snow is the best
Because it's lovely and white
Paper is white
It's lovely and bright
Paper is the best
Because it's white.

Rachel Connelly (7)
St Paul's CE Primary School, Sunderland

Dogs

A puppy goes *fast*
An old dog goes really *slow*
A puppy goes *yippy*
And old dog goes *oh no really slow*
A puppy goes *aaaahhhh*
An old dog goes *it's OK boy*
A puppy goes *come on*
An old dog goes *wait there son.*

Holly Telfer (7)
St Paul's CE Primary School, Sunderland

What Is Yellow?

The sun is bright
Daffodils are too
Fire is bright
Fireworks are at night
Bottles and bobbles are both the same
Yellow flags fly in the wind
Yellow makes me happy
And think of the sand.

Emma Goodrick (8)
St Paul's CE Primary School, Sunderland

Cat

My cat is fat
It eats rats
And the cat
Sits in the sink
And waits for snacks
The snacks are . . .
Rats!

Megan Hair (8)
St Paul's CE Primary School, Sunderland

What Is Blue?

Eyes are for seeing with
The sky is a friend to the sun
A blue tit is a bird which sings
A tear is sad
Fireworks are a big sparkle in the sky
A car zooms in the wind
Water sparkles in the sun
Bluebells are there to look at
See them bloom in the sun.

Levi Taylor (7)
St Paul's CE Primary School, Sunderland

Old Dog And Young Puppy

Old dog walks very, very, very slowly
Puppy whizzes by
Old dog can't run to the stick
Puppy whizzes by
Old dog so slow, so slow
Puppy whizzes by.

Michael Smith (8)
St Paul's CE Primary School, Sunderland

Cats

A kitten runs up and down,
An old cat doesn't run up and down,
He sleeps all day long.
I like kittens best,
They are cute and cuddly,
My kitten's name is Jerry,
I love my kitten.

Samantha McRoy (7)
St Paul's CE Primary School, Sunderland

Dogs

Old dogs are very weak
And can't run very fast
But puppies on the other hand
They're out like a flash
Fast dogs chase cats
And cats understand
Without dogs it wouldn't be
A very grand land.

Elliott Pratt (8)
St Paul's CE Primary School, Sunderland

The Pony

There was a little pony,
He lived in the stables,
He ate all the carrots
Like a little pony should.

He neighed at the lady,
He neighed at the baby,
He neighed at the man,
But he didn't neigh at me.

I knew I would have got left out,
But then the pony came.

He galloped by the lady,
He galloped by the baby,
He galloped by the man
And this time he galloped by me.

I was so happy,
I jumped with glee,
Now the pony belongs to me.

Natasha Little (11)
Stocksfield Avenue Primary School

Aliens Do Exist!

'Aliens don't exist!'
Most people say,
But I think they do,
In every way.

Why just last night
An alien landed
And spoke to me,
In an unknown language.

I got petrified,
I ran to tell my mum,
She just laughed and said,
'Don't be glum
Because *aliens don't exist!'*

Laura Gray (10)
Stocksfield Avenue Primary School

My Little Brother

My little brother
He has the most terrible habit
He jumps around like a rabbit

We had so much bother
Getting him to a doctor
The doctor said he was as fit as a fiddle
Right up to his middle
Oh bother
My little brother.

Bliss Jones (10)
Stocksfield Avenue Primary School

2 Cool 4 School

English and maths
I'm 2 cool 4 that
Science and RE
About 2 fall asleep under my hat

Music and PE
That's more like it
Handwriting and ICT
All day I sit and sit

Then comes playtime
That's what I love
Lunchtime and home time
Thank God above.

Lauren Walker (11)
Stocksfield Avenue Primary School

My Last Day Of School

Everyone was upset except me,
I didn't know why.
I was glad,
They were sad.

I didn't dare say,
Yes or hooray.

School had finally ended!
Everyone was glad,
So why was I so sad?

Ayesha Ali & Emily Rae (11)
Stocksfield Avenue Primary School

Alone

Beyond the grass,
Beyond the fields,
Beyond all the trees
Is where I sit, listening
To the sound of the whistling breeze.

The wind whips my hair,
It thrashes at my knees,
But I don't move a muscle,
Though I think that I might freeze.

No one knows this place but I,
The howling wind and stormy sky,
I sit alone with no company,
Not even a bird, flying high.

Kathryn Corner (10)
Stocksfield Avenue Primary School

A Bee

A bee flew after me
And that is why I flee, I flee.
I fled to Northern Africa
And back to Timbuktu
And all because a little bee
Tried to sting me,
(But never did.)

Bethany Parker (11)
Stocksfield Avenue Primary School

Animals

I am a kitten,
As fluffy as can be,
But if I get my claws out,
It's not a nice sight to see.

I am a puppy,
A little furry ball
And I am not a big pup,
I am actually quite small.

I am a foal,
I have a water trough,
I have a nice owner,
But I always chuck her off.

Danielle Whitlie (10)
Stocksfield Avenue Primary School

Someone's Nicked My Knickers!

Someone's nicked my knickers
And I just want them back,
When I find out who's nicked them,
I'll give them, I'll give them such a smack.

I left them in my cupboard
And they've just disappeared,
I can't believe they're gone,
This is so weird.

I can't go out with a bare behind,
I just wish it was all in my mind,
I better stop the moaning
Because I've just remembered I put them on this morning.

Laura Lawlor (11)
Stocksfield Avenue Primary School

Guess Who?

I'm orange and black,
I'm very fierce.
Still I look quite cute!
I live in the jungle.
Everyone is scared of me,
As my roar echoes.
Who am I?

I'm closely related to the tiger.
I have green bright eyes,
I Love to eat fish,
Such as tuna.
I'm a domestic house pet
And everyone loves me.
Who am I?

I live underwater,
With the fish and the crabs.
I am a mammal and I breathe air.
I bowride and dive
And show off my tricks
To passers-by.
Who am I?

I gallop and I canter,
Around the paddock.
I love to be ridden
And pampered
And brushed.
Who am I?

(Answers - a tiger, a cat, a dophin and a horse)

Rebecca Jordan (10)
Stocksfield Avenue Primary School

Without You

(To my cousin)

Without you I'm like
A ship with no sails,
A flower with no scent
Or animals with no tails.

Without you I'm like
A fish with no scales,
A dog with no bite,
Trees blown down by gales.

Without you I'm like
A giraffe with no neck,
A car without windows
Or a woodpecker with no peck.

Without you I'm like
A bird with no song,
A house without a roof,
A lane that never goes along.

Without you I'm like
A flower with no petal,
A car that is plastic
When it should be metal.

Without you I'm like
A car with no wheels,
A dog that needs to eat
But isn't given meals.

Scott Smithwhite (9)
Temple Park Junior School

Breakfast

Each day I crack my breakfast egg
I hope more and more
But one day when I crack it
Out will pop a dinosaur.

Laura Burns (9) & Anna Milburn (8)
Temple Park Junior School

Fog

I went outside into the fog,
I heard it speak,
'Be warned, young one!' it said.

I could see its white fingers,
Creeping around on the floor,
'Be warned, young one!' it said.

It was hiding things,
It drifted and rolled on the floor,
'Be warned, young one!' it said.

More and more looming shapes,
Cold and wet, damp and haunting,
'Be warned, young one!' it said.

It's a hooded creature,
Closing around me,
'Be warned, young one!' it said.

I ran home,
I don't like the fog,
I was warned!

Christopher Reay (11)
Temple Park Junior School

The Elephant Acrostic

E lephants, elephants have long trunks
L ots of them aren't smelly but some smell like skunks
E veryone likes elephants because they have big ears
P rotect yourself when they cry because they have big tears
H unger is a word the elephant won't use
A ll the time when he smells food, he will never refuse
N ow if you see an elephant then run far away
T hen shout, 'Goodbye, see you later and have a happy day.'

Karl Taylor (10)
Temple Park Junior School

Animals

A frican animals all on the field,
F ears leopards walking on the branch.
R ickity-rackity, the elephant is coming,
I vy honey guides picking a stick,
C atching beasts like leopards and elephants,
A nimals stomping on the hill,
N either of them can hide away.

A nimals always keep healthy,
N ear the trees we hear a rustle,
I magining there is someone there,
M eaningless birds all in their nest,
A ctive elephants thumping on the grass,
L ittle creatures crawling in the bush,
S ensible crawlies surrounding my feet.

Sophie Dickinson (9)
Temple Park Junior School

A Horse Called Shelley

My friend's horse called Shelley
has a liking for my wellies,
she bites my toes and licks my nose
when she lies next to her friend called Molly.
Her stable is cold and dreary,
but Shelley is always bright and breezy,
she runs through the fields
with the greatest of ease.
She then canters back,
quick as a flash
and snuggles down
for her sleep.

Melissa Beattie (9)
Temple Park Junior School

Colours

Blue is the colour of my coloured clothes,
They smell lovely upon my nose,
Soft and silky,
Smooth and twinkly,
That's the colour of my clothes.

Red is the colour of my smelly socks,
Kept in my room in a wooden box,
Rough and wrinkly,
Old and crinkly,
That's the colour of my socks.

Yellow is the colour of the noonday sun,
I think of it as I eat a bun,
Soft and silky,
Bright and twinkly,
That's the colour of the sun.

Helen Curry (11) & Savannah Hood (10)
Temple Park Junior School

African Animals

Lions weeping and sleeping
Tigers creeping and peeping
Zebras walking slowly
Cheetahs hunting sadly
Leopards eating happily
Elephants stopping and ripping trees down
Gorillas swinging tree to tree
Kangaroos jumping and hopping
Bulls charging madly
Bats sleeping and peeping through the clear air
Monkeys swinging from tree to tree.

Jessica White (9)
Temple Park Junior School

Harry Potter

Ron is a wizard,
Hermione is a witch,
Harry flies out to catch the Snitch.
Nimbus Two Thousand is Harry's broom,
When he plays Quidditch
Watch him zoom.

Snape teaches potions,
You better beware,
When I cast this spell
You'll get nightmares
Or you'll get zapped into a magic land,
Where all the funny monsters stare.

Hagrid leads you to the forbidden forest,
Dumbledore leads you down the hall,
Professor McGonagall says you're late,
Harry gives Hedwig a call,
Neville Longbottom loses his frog,
Harry and his friends get in a state.

Hagrid's dragon gives you a burn,
In flying lessons it's your turn,
Defence Against The Dark Arts,
Professor Quirrell takes part,
Draco Malfoy is slow to learn.

Sarah Wheeler (10)
Temple Park Junior School

Zebras

Z ebra's stripes are black and white
E ating is easy for zebras
B ecause they live in the wild
R eally fast to keep away from enemies
A good-looking animal, what do you say?

Jonathan Hoy (9)
Temple Park Junior School

Without You

(To my great nan)

Without you I'm like
A sun with no heat,
A horse with no mane,
Some shoes with no feet.

Without you I'm like
A shark with no bite,
A computer with no screen
And some string with no kite.

Without you I'm like
A boat with no sail,
A cat with no whiskers
Or fairies without a tale.

Without you I'm like
A tail with no wag,
A girl with my dolly,
That's why I'm so sad.

Without you I'm like
A sad, lonely child
Who misses so much
Your affection so mild.

Lauren Trotter (9)
Temple Park Junior School

The Honey Guide

Twirling and swirling up in the air
Dancing and prancing down on the ground
Sleeping and weeping on the branch
Flying and sighing up above
Dying and crying
Yet still what a beautiful sight.

Sophie Stewart (9)
Temple Park Junior School

Nature

Nature is beautiful
Nature is great
Nature is a thing someone must have made

All the birds a-singing
All the trees a-swaying
And also in the trees the children a-playing

It's so sad when you see
A man cutting down a tree
So tell them to stop a moment
And think of this poem

Nature is beautiful
Nature is great
Nature is a thing someone must have made.

Kristopher Spencer (11)
Temple Park Junior School

A Day At School

A day at school, Monday English and maths
It's boring, boring, I feel like snoring

A day at school, Tuesday, geography and topic
So you better not copy it

A day at school, Wednesday, science and art
So don't think you're so smart

A day at school, Thursday, computers and RE
So have a go and work out what you will be

A day at school, homework and extra play
After all my favourite day has got to be
Friday!

Samantha Wilson & Wendy Smith (9)
Temple Park Junior School

Without You

(To my friend)

Without you I'm like
A flower with no scent,
A star with no twinkle,
That's not what God meant.

Without you I'm like
A child who can't sing,
A cat with no purr
Or a bird with no wing.

Without you I'm like
Streets without names,
A dog with no fur,
We played some great games.

Without you I'm like
A fish with no fin,
A computer with no wires,
A goat scrambling in the bin.

Without you I'm like
A ship with no sea,
A dog with no name,
I just want it to be you and me.

Demi Turnbull (8)
Temple Park Junior School

Fire

There is a fire in the kitchen, can you see?
It's burning down the house, why me? Why me?
My cat will be frying up,
What about my nanny's pup?
The firemen came and put out the flame
And I got the blame.

Adam Tulloch (10) & Melissa Holmes (11)
Temple Park Junior School

Winter

Winter -
The best time of the year,
It's very cold and snow is falling,
Snowballs getting thrown by kids,
Smashing and crashing all over.

Winter -
The best time of the year,
Dressing up in warm clothes,
Woolly hats, scarves and gloves,
Drinking hot chocolate and other hot drinks.

Winter -
The best time of the year,
When Santa Claus comes,
He delivers all the presents,
To all the girls and boys.

Katie Lee (11)
Temple Park Junior School

My Favourite Things

One of my favourite things is the fog
Two of my favourite things is a dog
Three of my favourite things is art
Four of my favourite things is riding in a cart
Five of my favourite things is playing around

Six of my favourite things is speaking out loud
Seven of my favourite things is playing netball
Eight of my favourite things is being so small
Nine of my favourite things is my pet fish
Ten of my favourite things is ice cream lying in a dish.

Jessica Payne (10)
Temple Park Junior School

What Is . . . ?

What is my pet?
It's a grey and black friend.
It is a lovely fluffy pal,
Who is very soft and strokeable.

What is the moon?
It is a huge bristly thing in the sky.
It is a bouncy clay ball
That bounces far too high.

What is the sun?
It is a boiling pot of vegetable soup.
It is a juicy lollipop
That gets licked out of shape.

What is a star?
It is a gleaming point in the universe.
Could there be only one star out there?
It travels so high next to the moon.

What is a friend?
It is someone who cares for you.
It is someone who lets you play in their garden,
Sometimes they say, 'I am your friend.'

Abbie Dixon (7)
Temple Park Junior School

I Hate The Rain

Drip, drop
Drip, drop
When will the rain stop
So I can go out to play
And have a nice and funny day?
Drip, drop
Drip, drop.

Samantha Walker (9)
Temple Park Junior School

Without You

(My fish, Dipsy)

Without you I'm like
Some snow with no flakes,
A bird with no wings,
A car with no brakes.

Without you I'm like
A puddle that's dry,
A rainbow without colours,
A question without why.

Without you I'm like
Some seeds that can't grow,
A park with no swings,
Snowballs with no snow.

With no Dipsy I'm like
A swimmer that can't dive
A bowl with no fish
I wish you were alive.

Amy Sangster (8)
Temple Park Junior School

My Garden

I have a little garden
And all the grass is green,
There are plenty of yellow flowers
Bursting to be seen.

The fence is painted red,
To match the garden shed,
I love my little garden,
I can see it from my bed.

Rachel Kinvig (9)
Temple Park Junior School

Without You

(My dog, Buttons)

Without you I'm like
A star without light
Or a sun without its rays,
A white horse with no knight.

Without you I'm like
A cow with no calf,
Without you safe at home
My heart is split in half.

Without you I'm like
A bird with no wings
Or a fish that can't swim
Because it's got no fins.

Without you I'm like
Some grass with no deer
Or a window with no glass,
Buttons, I wish you were here.

Rebecca Mackley (9)
Temple Park Junior School

Best Mates

I have a little waggy tail
With two very deep blue eyes
A cold and little stubby nose
To make my masters sigh
I have two little floppy ears
A coat of brown and beige
A basket just for me to sleep
And dream away my days
My name is Bonnie, my friend is Skye
We go everywhere together
We share our masters through and through
We'll stay with them forever.

Anthony Jordan (9)
Temple Park Junior School

Untitled

The leopard
Searching and hunting for its prey
Pouncing and tearing its food for today
Sly and cunning as it moves its legs
Under the long grass is where the victim begs

The lion
Mane of a fire, teeth of a knife
In the jungle you plead for your life
Claws of a dagger, its fur silky smooth
Yawn the size of Saturn with the cat move

The giraffe
This herbivore creature with the neck of a tree
Is giant and beautiful and a great thing to see
The patches of Jupiter, the eyes of a star
They walk in the wild, a land of afar

The crocodile
Scales smooth and lumpy and has a nasty bite
Tail so massive and eyes glow at night
Large and fast reflexes, long snout and big teeth
Has this meat-eating animals that loves raw meat

The rhino
As he walks it's like a stampede this heavy herbivore makes
Plants, grass and bushes will settle his taste
You can hear him a mile off because of his heavy feet
This grey-skinned herbivore isn't interested in meat

The elephant
Grey big and loud, is the way this animals looks
Ears like big wings and great big white tusks
Skin of a rhino, trunk of a tree branch
This animal is gigantic, it only eats plants.

Lisa Bradwell (9)
Temple Park Junior School

What Is . . . ?

What is a star
So high in the sky?
It is a sparkling diamond
Baked in a jewel pie.

What is chocolate?
It is big, round and brown.
It could be a square bear
Owned by a clown.

What is a mountain?
It's a grey ice cream cone
And sometimes when its head is cold
You can almost hear it groan.

What is jelly?
Wibbly wobbly on your plate!
It looks like a squeezy fish
That can be your new mate.

What is a tree?
With fresh green leaves,
It could be a huge tuft of grass,
With branches that it heaves.

What is bubblegum?
It becomes a big, round balloon,
Watch out! Stand back!
It's going to *pop* soon!

Amy Cooper (8)
Temple Park Junior School

What Is . . . ?

What is a rainbow?
It is a coloured bit of Sellotape
To wrap up special presents,
It is a coloured smile upside down.

What is the wind?
It is an open mouth
Blowing the leaves off a tree,
It pushes the clouds in the sky.

What is the rain?
It is the water in the shower
Overflowing everywhere,
It is water sprinkling from a can.

What is a toadstool?
It is a fairy's house
In the middle of the wood,
It is a leprechaun's umbrella.

What is a Polo?
It is a plughole
And the water is escaping,
It is a minty hula hoop.

What is a star?
It is sequins on cloth
Glittering in the sky,
It is a silvery ball of gas.

Kate Fairhurst (8)
Temple Park Junior School

I Have A Dream . . .

I have a dream of a wonderful world
Without any litter
Without any graffiti
Where animals are not harmed
Where birds can fly freely

I have a dream
Where there is plenty of food for all
Where everyone cares for each other
Where there is no upset

I have a dream
Where there is no fighting and arguing
Where people share
Where everyone looks after each other

I dream of peace.

Bethany Collins (7)
Temple Park Junior School

What Is . . . ?

What is a rainbow?
A rainbow is like the letter 'n'
A rainbow has beautiful colours
It is friends with the rain

What is the moon?
It is a glittering, gleaming, white balloon
It is a squashy yellow banana
When it's a crescent in the heavens

What is the sun?
It is a yellow yolk in a powder-blue sky
It is a squeezy, rubbery ball
That bounces in the clouds.

Kristie Chambers (7)
Temple Park Junior School

What Is . . . ?

What is the moon?
It is a glittering, gleaming, white balloon,
It is a white golden banana
Floating in the sky day and night.

What is a rainbow?
It is a bright collection of colours in the sky,
It is a friend of the rain,
It shines over the pier and across the sea.

What is the star?
It is a twinkling, sparkling circle in the sky,
It is a happy fellow
Dancing in the sky.

What is a friend?
It is a kind person that looks after you
And cares for you,
They stop you from fighting and arguing,
That is a friend.

What is a dragon?
It is the breathing fire,
The hotness from the sun,
The burning breath from its mouth.

Hannah Dalton (8)
Temple Park Junior School

African Animals

A is for ant, as tiny as can be
F is for flamingo, smaller than a tree
R is for rhino with its very sharp horn
I is for in the forest where lions can roar
C is for cheetah that can run very fast
A is for animals, at home at last
N is for naughty, some elephants can be
stamping on plants and knocking over trees.

Charlotte Oakley (9)
Temple Park Junior School

What Is . . . ?

What is the sun?
It is a huge fried egg.
It is a hungry Cyclops' eye
Staring at your food.

What is a computer mouse?
It is a little mouse playing on the mat.
It is a mouse that scrolls up and down.
It's like a computer slave, that little mouse.

What is a worm?
It is a big long piece of slimy string.
It is a big piece of spaghetti
In a Bolognese sauce.

What is a video camera?
It is the head of a robot.
It is a picture camera
Taking pictures every second.

What is a pencil?
It is a big hard worm.
It is a thin paintbrush
Except it doesn't paint.

What is a shoe?
It is a laced-up spaceship.
It is a racing car
Brumming past the flag.

What is snow?
It is freezing cold powder blown up and down.
It is a bowl of white flowers
Getting thrown in the air.

Kieran Proctor (8)
Temple Park Junior School

I Have A Dream . . .

I have a dream of a beautiful world
Where no glass is broken or thrown around
Where no wildlife is destroyed
Where no trees are cut down
Where wild flowers can bloom

I have a dream where there is enough food for everyone
Where there is no sadness or dying
Where there is no hunger
Where everyone is loved

I have a dream where there is no fear
Where there is no hurt
Where there are no shotguns
Where there is no fighting

I dream of peace.

Charmaine Mitchell (7)
Temple Park Junior School

Untitled

One chubby hippo lying in the lake,
Two stripy zebras laughing at a snake.
Three white geese waddling around their home,
Four cute puppies munching on a bone.
Five little kittens purring very loud,
Six big lions feeling very proud.
Seven silly monkeys swinging from tree to tree,
Eight blue dolphins swimming in the sea.
Nine long lizards with their tongues sticking out,
Ten little hamsters scuttling about.

Ryan Ellison & Emily Smith (8)
Temple Park Junior School

At School

I'm running to school,
Don't want to be late,
Got to be there for nine,
Hoping everything is fine.

Got to keep on running,
Trying to look stunning,
My hair's flying all over,
Oh! I found a four-leaf clover.

I'm in the playground,
There is noise all around,
The teachers have come out,
They are beginning to shout.

I'm in the line,
Feeling fine,
Go to do my work,
To get home on time.

Mr Black is my teacher,
He teaches us sums, he is such a preacher,
But in the summertime we play games
And make funny frames.

Gemma Chandler (9)
Temple Park Junior School

Snow Time

As I sit in my room,
Looking out upon the gloom,
Snow is falling all around,
Covering every bit of ground.
I went to play with the other kids,
As snowball fighting is the craze.
My mam and dad won't let me play,
'Cause I am full of flu upon this day.
Until I'm better and feeling fine,
Snow will have to wait till another time!

David Steele (8)
Temple Park Junior School

Without You

(To my cousin)

Without you I'm like a ship with no sea,
But when we are together we have fun, you and me.
Without you I'm like a child with no love,
It's like seeing the pond without the dove.

Without you I'm like a street with no name,
Without you it all seems such a shame.
Without you I'm like a sky with no sun,
Without you I don't have very much fun.

Without you I'm like a homeless child,
Walking down the street, cold and mild.
Without you I'm like a fish with no scales,
Without you I'm like a boat with no sails.

Martin Stevenson (9)
Temple Park Junior School

Without You

(For my hamster, Fidget)

Without you I'm like
A child without a name,
I'm like a girl without a home
Or a fire without its flame.

Without you I feel like
I've lost part of my light,
You're not here to make me laugh
And I don't feel right.

Without you in your cage,
You're not here to hang around,
I used to love to watch you play,
But now you're buried in the ground.

Georgia Henderson (8)
Temple Park Junior School

Without You

(To my lost dog, Spike)

Without you I'm like
A garden with no dove,
A flower with no petals,
A heart with no love.

Without you I'm like
A seat with no chair,
A cup with no water,
A door that leads nowhere.

Without you I'm like
A field with no grass,
A plane with no wings,
A bus with no pass.

Without you I'm like
A sky with no sun,
A book with no pages,
A sandwich with no bun.

Without you I'm like
A hamster with no cage,
A train with no wheels,
A magazine with no funny page.

Without you I'm like
A horse with no knight,
A tooth with no gum,
You were my best dog, Spike.

Denise McKean (9)
Temple Park Junior School

What Is . . . ?

What is a cat?
It is a round, ginger ball.
It is a fluffy, golden pompom
That you can play with all day.

What is a camera?
It is a rectangular robot.
It is a square clicky box
That likes to wink at me.

What is fog?
It is a giant grey cloud.
It is damp fingers
That touch you on your shoulder.

What is the sun?
It's a giant gobstopper.
It is the sunny yolk of an egg
That's nice to dip your bread in.

What is a computer?
It is a large television eye.
It's a PlayStation that looks at me,
I wish I could play on it now.

What is a friend?
It is someone that's always there for me.
It is someone who is kind and gentle,
I think I have got one.

Lindsay Marshall (7)
Temple Park Junior School

Alphabet Poem

A is for Ann who is fat
B is for Ben who has a cat
C is for Claire who picks her nose
D is for Daniel who has 11 toes
E is for Emma who is kind
F is for Fred who is blind
G is for Georgia who is nasty
H is for Harry who eats a pasty
I is for Isabelle who is a frog
J is for James who plays with a log
K is for Katie who is a witch
L is for Liam who fell down a ditch
M is for Mary who is in Year 6
N is for Neil who eats breadsticks
O is for Olive who has no hair
P is for Paul who likes the fair
Q is for the Queen who is posh
R is for Robert who has lots of dosh
S is for Sarah who is good at writing poems
T is for Tom who lives in the hairy homes
U is for Ulrika who is a writer
V is for Victor who is a good fighter
W is for Wendy who is a waiter
X is a secret, I'll tell you later
Y is for Yolly who is tall
Z is for Zak who likes to fall.

Emma Barrow (10)
Temple Park Junior School

Habits

A is for Adam who can pull out two eyes
B is for Betty who can't stop eating pies
C is for Carl who keeps getting off his seat
D is for Daniel who eats Shredded Wheat
E is for Emma who is so nasty
F is for Fred who likes a cheese pasty
G is for Goldilocks who runs into people's houses
H is for Harry who has a voice like a mouse
I is for Isabella who talks far too much
J is for Jack who has a hard touch
K is for Katie who falls off her bike
L is for Laura who everyone likes
M is for Mary who picks her nose
N is for Nicola who has a bad pose
O is for Oscar who doesn't grow tall
P is for Pete who doesn't like the mall
Q is for the Queen who is very posh
R is for Rita who has lots of dosh
S is for Sarah, that's me
T is for Tom who buzzes like a bee
U is for Ulrika who is so nice
V is for Vivian who likes rice
W is for Wilma who has ginger hair
X is a secret but he's fat like a bear
Y is for Yasmin, she's a brat
Z is for Zak who has a funny hat.

Sarah Barrow (9)
Temple Park Junior School

What Is . . . ?

What is fog?
It is smoke that stops you see.
It is a grey balloon in the air
That I wish I could pop!

What is a star?
It is like a little spot that gleams in the sky.
It is a diamond sparkling bright.
It is a glittering speck in a field of blue
That really is a twinkle in the sky.

What is the sun?
It is a squeezy rubbery ball
That bounces in the sky.
It is a yellow smiley face.

Alix Deans (7)
Temple Park Junior School

Without A Friend

Without you I'm like
A car without a wheel
I'm like a house with no roof
Or a ship with no keel

Without you I'm like
A star with no light
I'm like the sun with no rays
Or a day with no night

Without you I'm like
A playground with no games
Because you're my very best friend
And I miss you, James.

Errol Kerr (8)
Temple Park Junior School

Leopard

L eopard leaps in a long jump,
E ager for his food, he hunts sneakily in the grass,
O ffends himself to keep him safe,
P ouncing everywhere, having fun,
A lways keeping healthy,
R eally fast to keep away from the hunters,
D ay ends; time to sleep, the morning is another day.

Charlotte Whittington (10)
Temple Park Junior School

Colours

Blue is the colour of my smelly socks
Where Nazis fly and bomb the docks

Yellow is the colour of my stripy T-shirt
Until I fall into the dirt

Red is the colour of our steaming sun
Where people boil until they are done.

Liam Airey (11)
Temple Park Junior School

Class Clown

I thought it would be good to be really daft
And so I did it for a laugh.
I acted the clown,
But I got a frown,
When the teacher said,
'Behave boy!'

George Allen (10)
Temple Park Junior School

Without You

(Friends far away)

Without you I'm like
A puppy with no home,
A body with no heart
Or a child with no bones.

Without you I'm like
A flower without a petal,
A snowflake on dry ground
Or a dry, steaming kettle.

Without you I'm like
A fish with missing gills,
A dog full of hunger
And I feel so dumb, dim and all alone.

Abbie Wales (8)
Temple Park Junior School

Giraffe

As it runs through the African grass,
Chased by a predator extremely fast,
Its tall next stretches out as it runs,
Giraffe gets away as tiger is stunned.
Giraffe prances to sit in the shade,
Then walks down to river to quietly bathe.
Lie on the bank with sun shining down,
Then see a lion so golden brown.
Hide in a bush coloured bright green,
Lion goes, nothing to be seen.
Giraffe comes out from bush,
Then walks across grass so lush.
Giraffe lies down for a rest,
As birds fly to their nice twig nest.

Lana Young (10)
Temple Park Junior School

Number Poem

One happy hyena trying to catch a cub,
Two drunken tigers coming out of a pub,
Three funky monkeys lying in bed,
Four mad dinosaurs, sorry but they're dead,
Five angry baboons jumping around their tree,
Six fast zebras eating a bumblebee,
Seven hairy gorillas banging on their chests,
Eight swarming mosquitoes wearing mini vests,
Nine hungry hippos going to the zoo,
Ten lazy zookeepers not going to the loo.

Steward Coates & Curtis Knowles (8)
Temple Park Junior School

If I Only Had . . .

I want a fluffy bunny
A fluffy ball of fun
I'd watch him hop
And run around
While sitting in the sun
He'd make me laugh
My bunny would
He'd make me cry with joy
If only I had a bunny
I'd be a very happy boy!

Laura Slesser (8)
Temple Park Junior School

What Is . . . ?

What is a bird?
It is a big, feather balloon
That will eventually come down
For me and you to keep.

What is a cat?
It is a ball of coloured wool,
It is a furry fluff-bag
That never stops playing.

What is a dragon?
It is a shape of green, fiery roughness,
It is a slice of smoky fire
That'll not stop moaning and groaning.

What is a toadstool?
It is a house for nice, pretty fairies,
It is a hideaway for goblins
Who are always up to nasty tricks.

What is an elephant?
It is a stomping grey shape,
It is a giant grey vacuum cleaner
That sucks up leaves and water.

What is a winter tree?
It is a mysterious shape,
It is a bony skeleton
That creaks and scares the passers-by.

Rachel Barry (7)
Temple Park Junior School

Glowing Moon

The moon is a crystal
The moon is like stars in the sky glowing at night
The big moon is like a ball looking at you when you're in bed
And make sure you're not scared
And the moon is not a balloon.

Farzana Ali (9)
Westgate Hill Primary School

Who Is The Moon?

The moon is bright
The glowing shadows dances on the moon
The moon is like sparkling glitter
And the moon is like a beautiful crystal ball in
The dark, gloomy night
Then the stars begin to shine
Now the stars are very light
Now the stars are going away
Then they say goodbye, goodbye.

Khadeeja Abbas (8)
Westgate Hill Primary School

Dragon's Supper!

A dragon is a scary thing,
It creeps and crawls for its prey
And when its prey is in sight,
It pounces and gives a frightful sight.
When his prey is shocked and stunned,
The dragon gives the meal no chance,
One, two, three chomps, bye bye,
It's goodnight.

Jordan Arkless (10)
Westgate Hill Primary School

March And April

March spring is very bright
It makes flowers smile
Spring makes people hot and sweaty

April is a shiny month
It makes the sky bright and shiny
April makes plants grow with the sun.

Joynal Ahmed (11)
Westgate Hill Primary School

Friendship

My friend, Nuru
Is like my very own guru

She sticks up for me
And I always go to hers for tea

Her house is nice and tidy
She likes my dog, Heidi

Her room is very messy
She has a doll called Jessy

She's like my twin
We stick together through thick and thin

I might go to the same secondary school
Her and I will be so cool.

Kali-Nammu Kisi-Songé (11)
Westgate Hill Primary School

What Is The Sun?

(Based on 'What Is The Sun?' by Wes Magee)

The sun is an orange dinghy
Sailing across a calm sea

It is a gold coin
Dropped down a drain in Heaven

It is a yellow beach ball
Kicked high into the summer sky

It is a red thumbprint
On a sheet of pale blue paper

It is a gold top from a milk bottle
Floating on a puddle.

Nazia Khatun (11)
Westgate Hill Primary School

A Bee Or Not A Bee

Aqua mail
Is it a whale
Coming far away from the sea?
Have you ever seen a whale
Coming closer to the bee?
A blue whale with water spraying
What a huge real deal!
Daddy was frightened
Of course it was only a joke
For children who are small
Just to have a laugh
Yellow is the colour of the bumblebee
Obviously it's flying
Over the sea
The bee is rocking and rolling
The whale is kicking and calling
Swimming through the water
Realistically
Asking the aquatics
If it will bite
The differences between the bumblebee
And the whale is in height
The whale is larger
And the bee is smaller
So which one do you think is taller?
A whale is a good swimmer
And a bee is a good stinger
So aqua mail
Now do you think it is a whale?
Yes but . . .

Kuhinoor Khanom (11)
Westgate Hill Primary School

The Moon Poem

The moon is big and great.
The moon is very bright.
The moon is sparkling like a star.
The moon is dazzling in the dark night.
The moon makes people happy.
The moon is very beautiful.
The moon is very calm.
The moon is very big.
The moon is bright and full of light.
The moon is very interesting.
The moon is sparkling in the night.
The moon is a big ball of light.
The moon is very peaceful.
The moon is very cheerful.
In the dark sky the moon shines brightly at night.

Sana-Ullah Tariq (9)
Westgate Hill Primary School

Poetry Rhyme

There is a girl called Khadeja
Who always wants to be a teacher
She is short
But really hates wearing shorts
She is tough
But really not rough
When she cries
She makes you want to die

Butterfly, butterfly
Your wings make me want to fly
Over my head you go
I really want to catch you, you know.

Susan Waringa (11)
Westgate Hill Primary School

The Shiny Moon

The moon is sparkling in the sky
Floating up there really high

The moon is bright and it's full of light

The moon is a big bulb that lights the dark sky
It fills me with joy

Some people think it's cheerful
Some people think it's sad

Some people think it's a normal moon
That helps us see in the night.

Rezwan Ahmed (8)
Westgate Hill Primary School

The Ball Of Light

The moon comes out beautifully like crystal
The moon is so bright, glowing at night
The enormous circle is sparkling
The moon's so plain, all happy and calm
The black dark night, the moon shines
The moon's shadows are always there
The moon is so white.

Hafsa Chowdhury (8)
Westgate Hill Primary School

Snowy Day

The snow is cold, I don't like it,
The trees look ugly and the owls are scared
And the footprints look gloomy.
The bats flew to the moon,
The smoke is coming out from that shed,
I just want the sun to come up again.

Ahmed Nabin (9)
Westgate Hill Primary School

Characters In Harry Potter

The dark Lord Voldemort
The terror of everyone's heart
Vandalising and killing was his sport
No mercy in his heart; no escape
A teacher was Albus Dumbledore to him

Powerful and majestic Albus Dumbledore
The headmaster of Hogwarts
Wisdom sat on his brow
His knowledge was great and seldom did he fail
His sight struck people with awe

The famous Harry Potter was parentless
An orphan at the hands of Muggles
His hair an unruly mess
A similar version of his father's
By Albus Dumbledore he was blessed

An excellent player at chess
Is red-haired Ronald Weasley
His family are the best
Fred and George are mischief makers
Which make them better than the rest

Clever bushy-haired Hermione Granger
When first arriving at Hogwarts
Was a stranger
Always top of the class
With Harry Potter she fought danger!

Afifah Chowdhury (11)
Westgate Hill Primary School

Winter Haiku

Snow falling gently
On top of houses for Christmas
Schools everywhere closed.

Sahara Choudhury (11)
Westgate Hill Primary School

The Bright Moon

The bright moon shines when you go to bed
When the curtains are open

The white moon has light shadows

The huge moon makes me cheerful
When I'm going to bed

When you sleep you can stand near the moon
And think about the sad things

I wonder what a wonderful day
When the moon sparkles at me.

Fatma Abuslaila (8)
Westgate Hill Primary School

The Cold Earth

The breath smashing in your face
Cold and windy, no one can stop
Blowing you away and things like trees
Swish, swoosh!
No one can stop
Scarves, hats, jumpers and gloves blowing away
And that was the end
Of the cold day!

Faheem Ahmed (9)
Westgate Hill Primary School

The Shining Moon

The moon looks like a crystal
The dazzling moon shines in the sky
The moon is shining in the dark sky
The moon glows in the dark
The moon makes you cheerful.

Shema Begum (8)
Westgate Hill Primary School

The Shimmering Moon

The moon is a sparkling ball of light,
It shines in the dark, dark night,
The moon glows at the top of the sky,
I wonder why the moon's so high?
It's a twinkling moon,
Not like a spoon,
It's just a dazzling crystal ball,
I'd love to ring the moon so high,
In the bright night sky,
I'd just love to have a ride on the moon
Or if I couldn't ride on it
I could at least touch it in the bright night sky.

Amina Begum (9)
Westgate Hill Primary School

The Sea

At night the sea rolls and barks,
Like wolves and dogs.
The sea may frighten things
Like little babies now,
The weeping waves carry boats,
Ships, beach balls, everything out to sea.

Nasir Ahmed (9)
Westgate Hill Primary School

The Devilled Moon

The moon sparkles in the night
The moon glows like diamonds flying around
The moon twinkles like emeralds
The moon lights the sky up like sapphires
The moon blinks at you like amethysts coming and going
The moon is always there.

Nazmul Rahman (9)
Westgate Hill Primary School

In Autumn

In autumn the leaves flutter
Down from the trees
The wind whistles
And the leaves crinkle
The colours change
To orange
To red
The sun sparkles
In the sparkling sky
In autumn the leaves change.

Jobah Samsunnahar (8)
Westgate Hill Primary School

In Autumn

In autumn the leaves change
To red, yellow and orange
In the sun the leaves shine, shine
And turn to yellow and gold
In the wind it whistles
In the wind it blows
And they flutter like colourful butterflies
In autumn the leaves change.

Najmine Begum (8)
Westgate Hill Primary School

Snowy Night

The bats are out
And the sky is white
Scared owls are having a fright
Steam from the chimney
Owls are scared
Owls are scared.

Sam Taylor (9)
Westgate Hill Primary School

Snowy Night

The moon shining like a diamond
How pretty it looks.
Rocks are becoming very big.
Snow looks so white
And sparkly it becomes.
Smoke from the houses looks like frightening ghosts.
Trees are coming alive.
Bats are saying goodbye
And going to sleep peacefully.

Ghosia Ismail (10)
Westgate Hill Primary School

Snowy Night

There once was a haunted house which nobody lived in
The door was tattered and was falling off its hinges
It was snowing thickly and the snow went inside the house
Owls and bats go inside the house to look for food
The trees look like humans with faces and hands
They look really scary
Bats and owls hibernating in the trees at wintertime
The snow was too much
That the trees were nearly sinking.

Mumena Ali (9)
Westgate Hill Primary School

Friendship

True friends are like diamonds,
They are safe and they care.
False friends are like leaves,
They leave you anywhere.

Your friend should be someone who cares
And who is always fair.

Bilkish Begum (9)
Westgate Hill Primary School

The Stormy Sea

Waves gushing across the sea
Rocks wet and covered in slime
Dead fishes smell very bad
Clouds moving side to side
Dark clouds gathered in one place
The sun rises from down to high
Waves crashing on rocks
Floating with the wind
Sea creatures lying dead
The sun rises from day to night.

Halima Khatun (9)
Westgate Hill Primary School

Aliens

Aliens are cunning, aliens are strange,
Aliens are outstanding and they can change.
One is contrary and one is afflicting,
But sometimes they're greenish and very differing.

Aliens are coming to discover Earth,
But they just want to fill their girth.
But really they are hypnotising everyone
And turning the Earth into a world of fun.

The Earth burst into little pieces
And the aliens burst into chemical and spices.

Muhammed Noor Ajwad Yusof (9)
Westgate Hill Primary School

El Campo Charro y la Cocina Vasca

DESDE MIS FOGONES

Pedro Montes González

Dedicado...

... a mi ama Josefa y a mi abuela Eladia.
"Vosotras sembrasteis las semillas de mi vida
y de mi amor por la cocina"

Introducción

No es posible resumir en un libro todas las recetas que abanderan platos tan completos o viandas tan deliciosas como las que nos ofrecen las gastronomías Salmantina y Vasca. Por eso en este libro recopilo algunas recetas que me he animado a reproducir en mis fogones, las que he memorizado en mi paladar con letras mayúsculas.

Algunos son platos clásicos que figuran en los más importantes tratados de cocina que he tenido la suerte de leer e interpretar. Otros son recetas que se han ido transmitiendo de generación en generación y que igualmente forman parte del recetario popular, tanto de Salamanca como de Euskal Herria.

Cuando me preguntan por mi origen suelo responder "*Mi padre es de Salamanca, mi madre de Palencia, se conocieron en el txitxarrillo de Barakaldo y me parieron en Sestao*". Por eso no es casualidad que haya elegido recetas de estos dos territorios, que han educado y enriquecido mi pasión por la cocina desde niño.

Vivir en Bizkaia me permitido degustar platos tan famosos como la merluza en salsa verde, el marmitako, la porrusalda, el besugo a la Bilbaína. Nacidos en algunos de los mejores restaurantes que tenemos la suerte de poseer.

Pero realmente si hay un elemento que fusiona perfectamente estas dos culturas gastronómicas es el Bacalao. Bilbao tiene una enorme tradición de buenos cocineros de bacalao probablemente desde el sitio a que fue sometido en las guerras Carlistas por el año 1835, cuando un comerciante bilbaino encargó por carta 100 ó 200 bacaladas, pero al acentuar mal la "o" en la petición, recibió 1.000.200 bacaladas. A aquel error tipográfico debemos agradecer, entre otros, el famoso bacalao al pil-pil, el bacalao a la bizkaina, al club ranero y otros muchos.

En Salamanca, la Iglesia medieval impuso los días de ayuno, con la abstinencia en Cuaresma durante casi la mitad de los días del año, quedando prohibido mantener relaciones sexuales y comer carne. El consumo de bacalao como alimento de calidad y barato, se disparó y se transformó en un icono religioso y de riqueza. Así, cuanto más viernes de ayuno había, más negocio para los principales proveedores de este preciado producto "los vascos".

De la cuaresma surgen recetas como las patatas con bacalao y arroz, el potaje de garbanzos de Pedrosillo ó de Fuentesauco con espinacas y bacalao También en ensalada con patata, huevo cocido, aceituna negra, aceite de oliva y pimentón, al Ajoarriero. Igualmente conocidas son las frituras como los "Soldaditos de Pavia", las croquetas y los buñuelos.

Otro elemento en común entre la gastronomía de Salamanca y Euskal Herria es la carne. En Bilbao tan importante como el bacalao es el "Txuletón" de vaca vieja, y si es de buey mejor. Se estila un corte de tres o cuatro dedos de sección. cocinados a la brasa "al punto" con un buen puñado de costrones de sal acentuando cada lasca.

Del Campo charro salen la D.O. Morucha recuperada hace años y la Ternera Charra, tiernas y de excelente calidad. Y por supuesto, su majestad el Cerdo ibérico, Secreto, Presa, Pluma, Solomillo... junto al gran elenco de embutidos de la tierra. Como dicen los lugareños, se aprovecha "hasta los andares" .

Estas dos culturas gastronómicas me han inspirado para hacer este recetario, un cuaderno de bitácora que habla del trabajo realizado durante años por nuestra gente.

Pedro MONTES

ensaladas

cremas y potajes

desde el mar

bacalao

¿y de postre?

unos vinos

para picar

Mousse de Piquillos

con bocado crujiente de Pato

Ingredientes

100gr de Piquillos, 6 dientes de ajo, 2 cucharadas de aceite de oliva, 1 dl de nata líquida, 1 hoja de gelatina, 100 gr de jamón de pato, 2 láminas de pan tostado por pintxo, sal y pimienta.

Elaboración

Pochar los ajos laminados en aceite de oliva, retirar la mitad cuando empiecen a coger color y reservar. Añadir los pimientos de piquillo y sazonar con sal y azucar. Rehogar a fuego lento durante 10 minutos, añadir el caldo y la nata líquida, cocer 5 minutos más, triturar y colar fino. Poner la gelatina a remojo en agua fría y añadir a la crema en caliente, rectificar de sal, enfriar y reservar. Batir la clara de 2 huevos a punto de nieve e incorporarle muy suave la crema de piquillos. Montar bocaditos con 2 lonchas finas de pan tostado y una loncha de jamón de pato.

En un vasito pequeño poner la espuma de piquillos hasta el borde, disponer encima una lámina de ajo y un bocadito de pato

Mousse de Foie

y confitura de naranja

Ingredientes

50 gr. de mermelada de naranja, 150 gr de micuit de foie, 1/2 vaso de caldo vegetal o de agua templada, Sal, Azúcar, Pimienta y 1 dl de Pedro Ximénez.

Elaboración

Batir el foie y añadirle, el caldo, la sal, azúcar y pimienta. Batir a baja potencia para que no se corte el foie por aumento de temperatura. Introducirr en una manga pastelera y reservar en la nevera hasta que lo usemos. Sacar una hora antes de su uso para poner a temperatura ambiente.

Para la resentación, colocamos los vasitos y ponemos 2 o 3 cucharadas de café de mermelada, encima el doble de mousse de foie, adornar con frutos secos, virutas de jamón, etc. Rematar el chupito con un poco de reducción de Pedro Ximenez.

Boquerones al Ajillo

con aceite de oliva virgen extra

Ingredientes

1 kg de boquerones medianos, zumo de 2 limones, aceite de oliva, guindilla, ajo y perejil

Elaboración

Limpiamos los boquerones y sacamos los lomos procurando retirar bien todas las espinas.

Para cocinar los boquerones utilizaremos el ácido del zumo de dos limones más dos medidas iguales de agua. Dejamos que los boquerones se maceren en esta solución entre durante 45 minutos y 1 hora.

Para el aliño, picamos muy fino un manojo de perejil, picamos tambien 2 dientes de ajo y unos aros de guindilla, los salteamos en una sartén con aceite de oliva hasta que comiencen a dorarse, retiramos y dejamos enfriar.

Para la presentación, en una fuente hechamos un buen chorro de aceite de oliva virgen extra y la extendemos por todo el fondo. Colocamos los lomos por toda la fuente y con una cuchara cubrimos con el sofrito con ajo que habíamos dejado enfriar.

Bacalao al Ajillo

con aceite de oliva virgen extra

Ingredientes

250 gr. de lomos de bacalao desalado, Aceite de Oliva Virgen Extra, ajo y perejil.

Elaboración

Desalamos los lomos de bacalao (durante 36 horas cambiando 3 veces de agua y siempre en la nevera). Troceamos en cuadrados de 2,5 centímetros. Ponemos una cazuela con agua a hervir, cuando llegue a punto de ebullición asustamos los trozos de bacalao durante 15 segundos, rápidamente los sacamos e introdudimos en un recipiente con agua fría para que corte la cocción. Colocamos el bacalao en papel secante y reservamos.

Picamos muy fino 2 ó 3 dientes de ajo y los salteamos en una sartén con aceite de oliva a fuego medio hasta que se doren. Retiramos y dejamos enfriar.

Para la presentación, hacemos brochetas con 3 trozos de bacalao, las ponemos en una fuente y cubrimos con el aceite y los ajos. Por último espolvoreamos un poco de perejil picado.

Salmón ahumado relleno

de queso philadelfia y eneldo

Ingredientes

250 gr. de Salmón Ahumado loncheado, 100 gr de queso Philadelphia , eneldo y Aceite de Oliva Virgen Extra.

Elaboración

Cogemos una cucharada de café, de queso de untar y la colocamos sobre cada loncha de salmón ahumado, formamos rollitos más o menos de bocado. Los colocamos sobre una fuente y espolvoreamos con unas hebras de eneldo

Presentar con un chorrito de Aceite de Oliva Virgen Extra. También se puede espolvorear un poco de crujiente de cebolla confitada.

Anchoas en Salazón

Tostada, piquillo y crujiente de cebolla

Ingredientes

150 gr de anchoas en salazón, pimientos de Piquillo, Tostadas de pan, cebolla confitada, aceite de oliva, ajo y perejil

Elaboración

Congelamos las anchoas 24 h. para prevenir del anisaquis. Una vez descongeladas limpiar de cabeza y tripas, dejar la espina central para que no se estropeén. En un recipiente con tapa y agujero en el fondo (para que los líquidos que sueltan vayan saliendo), ponemos una cama de sal, otra de boquerones y cubrir con más sal, dejar 1 cm entre ellos. Prensar un poco con la ayuda de otro recipiente. así hasta terminar todas las anchoas. Meter en la nevera 1 mes mes y medio e ir sacando según se necesiten. Limpiar la sal y quitar las espinas.

Para el aliño, picamos muy fino un manojo de perejil, picamos tambien 2 dientes de ajo, los salteamos en una sartén con aceite de oliva hasta que comiencen a dorarse, retiramos y dejamos enfriar. Cubrimos con el refrito las anchoas.

Para la presentación, en una fuente hechamos un buen chorro de aceite de oliva virgen extra y la extendemos por todo el fondo. Colocamos los lomos por toda la fuente y con una cuchara cubrimos con el aceite con ajo que habíamos dejado enfriar.

Hornazo

Charro

Ingredientes

Para la masa:

1 kg de harina, 1 vaso de vino blanco, 1 vaso de aceite de oliva, 1 vaso de leche, 3 huevos, 25gr de levadura prensada, sal y azafrán.

Para el relleno:

lomo adobado, chorizo cular en rodajas gruesas, jamón serrano y huevo duro (opcional).

Elaboración

Deshacemos la levadura y la sal en el vaso de vino blanco, en un recipiente echamos los huevos, la mezcla del vino, y el aceite, lo mezclamos todo bien, vamos incorporando la harina poco a poco y el azafrán, removiendo bien hasta obtener una mezcla que no se pegue en los dedos, la amasamos y la dejamos reposar tapada con un paño húmedo.

Pasadas al menos 2 horas, estiramos la masa dejandola muy fina, 3mm más o menos, cortamos dos partes iguales. Colocamos una en la bandeja de horno, encima de un papel vegetal para que no se pegue, y sobre la masa vamos poniendo, una 1ª capa con los filetes de lomo crudos, otra con las rodajas de chorizo, encima el jamón en lonchas no muy finas, y por último el huevo cocido el rodajas , lo tapamos con la otra parte de la masa, cerramos bien los bordes, y lo pinchamos con un tenedor, pintamos con huevo batido y lo metemos en el horno precalentado durante 40 min. apróximadamente a unos 200º.

Buñuelos
de Bacalao

Ingredientes
150 grs de bacalao desmigado y desalado, 1 Patata, 1 Diente de ajo, 1 Huevo, 1/2 cebolla o cebolleta, 150 cc de agua, 120 grs de harina común, Una pizca de colorante, Una cucharadita de levadura, Sal y perejil picado, Aceite de oliva para freír.

Elaboración
Ponemos en un cazo agua a calentar, cocer la patata pelada y troceada durante unos 10 minutos. Casi al final de la cocción le añadimos el bacalao (sin espinas), Dejar unos 10 minutos a fuego medio. Cuándo la patata y el bacalao, estén blanditos, sacar con una espumadera, y reservar en un plato (Guardar el agua del bacalao).

Desmigar el bacalao en un bol y aplastar junto a la patata con un tenedor. Aañadir el resto de los ingredientes. Batimos el huevo ligeramente y lo introducimos. Agregar el ajo, la cebolleta y el perejil todo muy picado. Añadir una pizca de colorante alimenticio, un poco de sal al gusto, la harina, la levadura y finalmente el agua de la cocción del bacalao. Mezclamos muy bien todo hasta formar **una** pasta ligera "como una papilla".

Freir en abundante aceite hasta que estén dorados por ambos lados, sacar y dejar en un papel de cocina, para quitar el exceso de aceite.

Croquetas
de Farinato

Ingredientes
1/2 litro de leche
3 cuch.de harina
un tozo de farinato
sal
huevo
pan rallado
Aceite de Oliva.

Elaboración
Deshacer el farinato en una sarten con una cucharada de Aceite de Oliva, añadir la harina. Se formará una pasta que debe cocinarse bien para que no sepa a harina cruda. Vamos incorporando la leche poco a poco sin dejar de remover, ponemos a punto de sal. Cuando la masa se despegue de la sarten, la ponemos en un bol o en una manga pastelera. Dejar que se temple y por último damos forma a las croquetas .

Rebozar las croquetas primero en harina, después pasar por el huevo y por último por el pan rayado.

Freir en aceite abundante.

Timbal de Huevos rotos

Patatas y Farinato

Ingredientes

Para 2 personas: 2 huevos, 100 grs de farinato, 1 patata median, aceite de oliva virgen extra, pimienta y sal

Elaboración

Pelamos la patata y la partimos en rodajas finas. La freímos en una sartén con abundante aceite caliente.

Cortar dos rodajas de 1 centímetro de farinato, aplastarlo un poco y cocinarlo en la plancha sin aceite hasta que veamos que se dora. Lo sacamos de la sartén, retiramos la piel y reservamos.

Una vez fritas las patatas escurrir bien y salpimentar, no tienen que quedar aceitosas.

Freír los huevos.

Para emplatar mezclamos las patatas y el farinato. Añadir los huevos fritos a la mezcla y "rompérlos" con ayuda de un cuchillo y un tenedor. Mezclar un poco.

Con la ayuda de un molde, rellenar con la mezcla, prensar un poco y servir.

Hongos
con Foie

Ingredientes

Para los hongos:
500 grs de hongos, 2 chalotas, aceite de oliva, sal y pimienta.

Para el Foie:
8 escalopes de foie gras, sal en escamas, pimienta,

Elaboración

Limpiamos los hongos con un paño, y el pié lo pelamos con un pelador de patatas. Se hace mejor y estropeamos menos carne. Lo podemos hacer con una puntilla bien afilada.
Si el hongo está recién cogido y sano, no hace falta quitarle las "laminillas" que tiene debajo del sombrero. Pero si se las queréis quitar, las quitáis.
Partimos los hongos en trozos no muy pequeños, para que después de cocinarlos "tengan mordida", ya que al cocinar se deshidratan, y encogen.
En una cazuela, ponemos aceite de oliva suave y añadimos las chalotas cortadas en juliana fina.
Rehogamos las chalotas un par de minutos y añadimos los hongos. Salpimentamos. Vamos dando vueltas para que se vayan haciendo. En diez minutos más o menos estarán listo.
Probamos y a la hora de emplatar podemos añadir sal en escamas.

ensaladas

Ensalada de Bacalao
y tapenade de oliva negra

Ingredientes
200 gr. de migas de bacalao desalado, 100 gr de aceitunas negras, 2 cucharadas de salsa de tomate, bouquet de lechugas, Aceite de Oliva Virgen Extra, sal y vinagre de modena.

Elaboración
Tapenade de aceituna negra; batir un puñado de aceitunas sin hueso, un chorrito de aceite de oliva virgen y una cucharada de agua, hasta obtener una pasta cremosa.

Para el bacalao, doramos un diente de ajo picado muy fino en un chorro de aceite de oliva a fuego lento cuando empiece a dorar retirar del fuego y dejar enfriar. Hacer hebras con la migas de bacalao y mezclar con los aceite de ajos.

Seleccionamos algunas hojas de varias lechugas cortamos en trozos pequeños y aliñar con aceite y vinagre de módena, salpimentar.

Para montar los vasitos de ensalada; ponemos una cucharada de tomate en el fondo, cubrimos con una capa de bacalao, encima extendemos un poco de tapenade de aceitunas y cubrimos con el buquet de lechugas.

Perdiz escabechada

setas y aceitunas

Ingredientes

1 Perdiz, 2 dientes de ajo, 1 Hoja de Laurel, 1 Clavo, 1 Rama de Tomillo, 1 Cebolla, 1 Zanahoria, 1 Taza de Aceite de Oliva, 1/2 Taza de vinagre de Jerez, 1 Vaso de vino blanco, sal y pimienta.

Para las Setas:

Champiñones, Setas de cardo, 2 dientes de ajo, 1 nuez de mantequilla, 2 cucharadas de aceite de oliva virgen extra, perejil, sal y pimienta

Elaboración

Para el escabeche, limpiar bien la perdiz, quemando las plumas y sazonar. Dorar en una sartén con aceite de oliva a fuego medio.

En una cazuela saltear ligeramente los dientes de ajos, la cebolla y la zanahoria. Añadir el clavo, el laurel, el tomillo, el vino blanco, el vinagre y el aceite. Dejar cocer durante una hora, hasta que estén tiernas.

Saltear las setas picadas, en una sartén con la nuez de mantequilla y 2 cucharadas de aceite de oliva añadir 1 diente de ajo y el perejil picado, reservar.

Montamos la ensalada, colocando en la base del plato un bouquet de lechuga, encima unas pocas de setas. Ponemos media perdiz sobre las setas, añadimos unas aceitunas y aliñamos con la salsa del escabeche.

Ensalada de Regajo

Ingredientes

200 gr de Regajo, 2 dientes de ajo, Aceite de Oliva Virgen Extra, Vinagre y sal.

REGAJO (STELLARIA MEDIA)

También conocido como: "alsine", "pamplina", "lapilla", "hierba gallinera", en Asturias, "meruxa". En Euskal Herria "sapabelarr" o sea "hierba de sapos". En Galicia, "morugen". Es una planta de pequeñas hojas ovaladas siempre verdes, de flor blanca. Se cria en riberas, arroyos y lugares donde hay corrientes de agua. Cuando se va secando el cauce de los regatos, el regajo también se seca. De gran uso en gastronomía de algunos restaurante salmantinos de alto copete. Hay que escoger las hojas con sumo cuidado pues suele estar mezclado con ovas y otras hierbas que no son comestibles y sí algo indigestas.

Elaboración

El Regajo hay que escogerlo bien, separando hierbas y otras impurezas que se unen al recogerlo. Se debe lavar meticulosamente unas tres veces. Una vez limpio se dipone en una ensaladera.

Para el aliño: picamos los 2 dientes de ajo muy fino. En un mortero preparamos un majado incorporando 3 cucharadas de aceite de oliva y una de vinagre, ponemos a punto de sal y aliñamos la ensalada.

Cogollos de Tudela

Ventresca de bonito, piquillos y anchoas

Ingredientes

2 Cogollos de Tudela por comensal, 1 lata de anchoas, 1 lata de ventresca, 2 pimientos de piquillo por comensal, 1 cebolleta, 1/2 huevo duro por comensal, aceite de oliva virgen extra, vinagre balsámico de módena y sal.

Elaboración

Cortamos los cogollos en 4 y cubrimos el fondo en forma de estrella. Sacamos lascas de la ventresca y las ponemos encima ó junto a los cogollos, encima colocamos los pimientos de piquillo y los filetes de anchoa.

Repartimos por el plato el huevo cocido cortado en cuartos, También una cebolleta cortada en juliana.

Aliñamos la ensalada con 2 cucharadas de aceite de oliva virgen extra (variedad Arbequina), 1 cucharada de vinagre de módena y ponemos a punto de sal.

Limón Serrano

Ingredientes

8 naranjas, 4 limones, 4 huevos cocidos, 200 gr de chorizo cular ó jamón serrano, 200 gr de carne (secreto ibérico, entrecot de ternera, 1 diente de ajo, 2 ramas de perejil, una cucharada de aceite de oliva virgen extra, 1/2 cucharada de vinagre, sal y pimienta

Elaboración

Salpimentamos la carne (que puede ser de secreto, solomillo de cerdo o de ternera) y la braseamos en una sartén a fuego fuerte.

Pelamos los limones y las naranjas, se cortan en rodajas finas.

Se cuecen los huevos y se cortan en trozos, mezclándolos con las naranjas, los limones, el chorizo cortado a rodajasy la carne desmenuzada (*podemos saltear el chorizo. también se puede optar por jamón en vez de chorizo*) .

Se hace un machado en el mortero de ajo, perejil, aceite, vinagre y sal. Esta mezcla se remueve y se vierte sobre las naranjas y limones. Se mueven hasta que cojan el sabor y se sirve frío.

cremas y potajes

Crema de garbanzos
con foie fresco y setas

Ingredientes

1/2 kg de garbanzos de Pedrosillo, 1 carcasa de pollo, 1 puntita de jamón serrano, 1 hoja de laurel, 1 cebolla roja, 1 puerro, 2 dientes de ajo, Foie fresco, Setas, Aceite de Oliva, sal y pimienta.

Elaboración

Para los garbanzos, tras haberlos dejado a remojo desde la víspera, los ponemos a cocer a en una olla a presión, durante 30 minutos, junto con el puerro, la cebolla, el ajo, el laurel, la carcasa de pollo y la punta de jamón. Una vez cocidos trituramos con parte del caldo hasta conseguir una ligera crema. Reservamos.

Salteamos unas setas picadas en cuadraditos con una cucharada de aceite de oliva, 1 diente de ajo picado, 1 chorrito de Armagnac, sal y perejil. Reservamos.

Montamos el plato pomiendo un cazo de crema en el fondo, seguido colocamos 1 cucharada de setas cruzando el plato y por último una rodaja de Foie fresco salteado en plancha fuerte 15 segundos por cada lado. Terminamos con un pellizco de sal maldón sobre el Foie. y un chorrito de Aceite de Oliva Virgen Extra sobre los Garbanzos.

Porrusalda

albondigas de bacalao y pil pil de pimentón

Ingredientes

400 gr de Puerros, 250 gr de patata roja, 2 zanahorias, 2 dientes de ajo, 200 gr de Bacalao desmigado desalado, Aceite de Oliva, harina, un huevo, pimentón y sal.

Elaboración

Limpiamos bien los puerros y las zanahorias, pelamos y tronchamos las patatas y los ponemos a cocer en una olla expréss durante 30 minutos, junto con 2 dientes de ajo, un chorro de aceite de oliva, laurel y el punto de sal. Cubriendo todo de agua. Una vez cocido, escurrimos y trituramos añadiendo el caldo necesario hasta conseguir una crema ligera. Resevamos.

En una sartén con una cucharada de aceite, salteamos el bacalao durante 5 o 10 minutos con un ajo picado. desmenuzamos el bacalao con un tenedor, hacemos pequeñas albóndigas y las enharinamos. Freímos y reservamos.

Con pieles y espinas de bacalao, aceite de oliva y un par de dientes de ajo hacemos un pil-pil, añadimos una cucharadita de pimentón y reservamos.

Montamos el plato cubriendo de porrusalda, decoramos con 6 albondiguas por persona y matizamos con el pil-pil de pimentón.

Patatas meneás

ó patatas revolconas

Ingredientes

1,5 kilos de patata roja, 200 gr de torreznos, 1 pimiento rojo, 1 cebolla mediana, 6 dientes de ajos rojos, 2 hojas de laurel, Aceite de oliva virgen extra, Sal gruesa y pimentón.

Elaboración

Pelar y cortar las patatas en trozos para cocerlas en agua con un poco de sal gruesa, un pimiento rojo en trozos que posteriormente retiraremos, y dos hojitas de laurel fresco. Cuando las patatas estén cocidas se retira el caldo y se reserva. Comenzamos a machacar las patatas con un tenedor y también las reservamos.

Mientras se cuecen las patatas se va friendo la panceta. En la grasa que ha soltado se pochan lento la cebolla y los ajos a fuego lento. Añadir un poquito de caldo de la cocción de las patatas y triturar con la batidora. La salsa resultante la incorporaremos sobre las patatas que previamente ya hemos machacado con un tenedor. Continuaremos machacando las patatas mezclándolas con la salsa, añadiendo caldo hasta obtener la textura que deje ver trozos de patata. Añadir un poquito más de pimentón dulce ó picante al gusto.

Lentejas de la Armuña

con bacalao al Pil pil y costrones ibéricos

Ingredientes

Para las lentejas: 1/2 kg de lentejas de la armuña, 1 cebolla roja, 1 puerro, 1 trozo de hueso de jamón, 2 dientes de ajo, agua o caldo de pollo, 1 hoja de laurel y sal.

Para el bacalao: 2 lomos de bacalao desalado, 1/4 ltr. de aceite de oliva virgen extra, 2 dientes de ajo.

Para los costrones: 25 gr. de grasa de jamón o paleta ibérica, 4 rebanadas de pan tipo pistola, aceite de oliva virgen extra y sal.

Elaboración

Ponemos a remojo las lentejas en víspera. En una cazuela rápida rehogar en un chorro de aceite, 2 dientes de ajo, la cebolla y el puerro todo picado. Añadimos el hueso de jamón. incorporamos las lentejas, la hoja de laurel y ponemos a punto de sal. Cubrimos con el agua o el caldo. Tapamos y guisamos durante 1 hora a fuego medio. Triturar y pasar por el chino

Para los costrones, cortamos en cuadraditos pequeños el pan. En una sartén deshacemos la grasa de ibérico, con 2 cucharadas de aceite de oliva y removemos el pan hasta que se haya dorado, retiramos a un papel secante y reservamos.

Para el bacalao, ponemos a fuego medio una cazuela con el aceite y los ajos, cuando bailen en la superficie, retiramos 2/3 del aceite y los ajos e incorporamos el bacalao, bien seco y con la piel hacia arriba. cuando cojan calor, retiramos la cazuela del fuego y meneamos incorporando el aceite hasta ligar el aceite y la gelatina. Reservamos.

Presentación: cubrir el fondo con la crema de lentejas, sacar lascas de bacalao y rellenar el centro haciendo una rosa, decorar con los costrones y salsear con el pil pil.

Pardinas (Alubia blanca)

con almejas

Ingredientes

500 gr de judias blancas cocidas, 500 gr de almejas, 2 pimientos verdes, 1 cebolla, 4 cucharadas de salsa de tomate, un vaso de vino Arribes de Vetonia blanco, 3 dientes de ajo, pimentón dulce, 2 vasos de caldo de pescado ó agua, perejil, 1 hoja de laurel, aceite de oliva vrigen extra y sal.

Elaboración

Pochamos la cebolla y el pimiento picados en una cazuela con aceite y un poquito de sal. agregamos el ajo picado, y el laurel cuando empiece a dorar añadimos dos cucharadas de pimentón y la salsa de tomate, rehogamos 4 ó 5 minutos y reservamos.

En una sartén abrimos las almejas con un poco de aceite y reservamos.

Añadimos las judías cocidas al sofrito junto con el vaso de vino y el caldo. Removemos y dejamos guisar durante 10 ó 15 minutos.

Incorporamos las almejas con el caldo que han soltado al abrirse, Dejamos hervir 5 minutos y espolvoreamos el perejil picado por encima.

desde el mar

Besugo Asado
a la Bilbaína

Ingredientes

1Besugo de 1,5 kg, 1/2 vaso de Txakoli, aceite de oliva virgen extra, vinagre de Jerez, 4 dientes de ajo, 1 guindilla, perejil y sal.

Elaboración

Limpiamos el besugo, quitando escamas, coagulos y otras impurezas. Lo abrimos en libro pero sin quitar la espina, pues servirá de referencia para saber si está hecho. Ponemos el pescado en una bandeja, Lo rociamos bien con sal por dentro y por fuera. Introducir 10 ó 15 minutos en el horno a 180º. Cuando al tirar de la cabeza hacia atrás, casca con facilidad, el pescado está en su punto. Presentamos en una bandeja.

Picamos los ajos y lel perejil, troceamos en rodajas la guindilla (*que el picante no nos estropee el plato*) y reservamos.

En abundante aceite sofreímos los ajos y dos rodajas de guindilla procurando dorar poco a poco, rociar el besugo. Volcar de nuevo el líquido con los jugos del besugo en la sartén a fuego vivo, añadir un chorro de vinagre, menear bien para que emulsione todo y volver a rociar el besugo. Repetir de nuevo esta operación y servir.

Marmitako

receta de Ondarroa

Ingredientes

1 kilo de lomo de bonito del norte, 2 zanahorias, 4 patatas grandes, 3 cebollas moradas de Zalla, 1 tomate, 2 puerros, caldo con espinas y recortes de carne de bonito, 1 pimiento rojo, 1 pimiento verde, 500 grs. de tomate frito casero, 4 cucharadas de carne de pimiento txoricero, 1 copa de txakoli, 1 trozo de pan duro, sal gorda.

Elaboración

Preparar un caldo cociendo durante 1 hora, las espinas y recortes del bonito, 1 cebolla, 1 puerro, 1 zanahoria, 2 dientes de ajo, unos granos de pimienta y sal. Cubrir con 1 1/2 litro de agua.

Cortamos muy fino, los dientes de ajo, el pimiento rojo, el pimiento verde, la cebolla morada de Zalla y ponemos en una olla grande, con unas cucharadas de aceite de oliva virgen extra, y dejamos pochando la verdura a fuego medio (3/6) durante 1 hora y media. Cuando esté bien pochado le añadimos una copa de txakoli. Pelamos la patata y la rompemos. Removemos bien durante 15 minutos todos los ingredientes. Añadimos un trozo de pan duro. Añadimos el tomate frito casero y removemos. Añadimos el caldo de pescado poco a poco durante la cocción. Incorporamos al guiso la pulpa de los pimientos choricero, ponemos a punto de sal.

Cortamos los lomos de bonito en dados. Ponemos a calentar la sartén a fuego alto (5/6) con una gota de aceite de oliva virgen extra. Damos un toque de sal gorda a los dados de bonito los marcamos unos segundos con un puñado de perejil picado, lo incorporamos a la cazuela con el resto, retiramos del fuego y dejamos que repose con el bonito 5 minutos.

Merluza
en salsa verde

Ingredientes

1 Merluza fresca de 1 kg, almejas, espárragos, guisantes, 2 huevos cocidos 2 dientes de ajo, 1/2 vaso de txacoli, harina, perejil, aceite de oliva, sal y pimienta.

Elaboración

Desescamaos la merluza y la limpiamos bien de impurezas. Guardamos la cabeza para otras elaboraciones y con el resto hacemos rodajas de unos 2 cm. La salamos y pasamos por harina. Marcamos todos los pedazos en una sartén con un poco de aceite y reservamos.

Rehogamos en una cazuela con un chorro de aceite de oliva los dientes de ajo a fuego lento. Cuando empiecen a dorarse añadimos una cucharada de harina y removemos bien, añadimos el txakoli y subimos la temperatura del fuego hasta que se evapore todo el alcohol. Añadimos el perejil y vamos incorporando el agua de los espárragos hasta conseguir una salsa verde claro.

Agregamos la merluza a la salsa, añadimos los guisantes y los espárragos. Meneamos bien para que emulsione la salsa hasta lograr una textura similar al pil pil. Por último partimos los huevos cocidos en cuartos y decoramos.

Sopa de Pescado

receta de Ondarroa

Ingredientes

100 gr. de pimiento verde, 100 gr. de pimiento rojo, 100 gr. de cebolla, 100 gr. de puerro, 200 gr. de tomate triturado, 300 gr. de pescado blanco, 200 gr. de gambas, 200 gr. de almejas, 2 huevos cocidos, 2 dientes de ajo, 1 hoja de laurel, 1,5 litros de agua, Aceite de oliva, sal y pimienta, 1 guindilla de cayena y Perejil fresco

Elaboración

Hacer un caldo con 1/2 cebolla, 1/2 puerro, la piel y las espinas del pescado y las cabezas de las gambas. Reservar.

Poner una sartén con aceite y saltear los ajos, la cebolla, el puerro y los pimientos, todo muy picado, a fuego medio durante 1 hora, removiendo bien, hasta que tome un color dorado. Añadir la salsa de tomate y un chorrito de txakolí. Saltear otros 10 minutos y añadir el caldo. Dejar que cueza otros 20 minutos, añadir el pescado en trozos medianos. Reservar en la sopera.

Abrir las almejas en una cazuela con aceite y ajo picado y un trozo de guindilla. Conforme se vayan abriendo agregar a la sopera. Saltear las colas de las gambas peladas unos segundos y añadir a la sopera.

Picar fino 2 huevos cocidos agregar a la sopa y espolvorear perejil.

Txipirones (Begi haundi)
en su tinta

Ingredientes
12 txipirones frescos, 2 sobres de tinta, 2 cebolletas, 1 cebolla roja, 2 dientes de ajo, salsa de tomate, 1/2 kg de arroz bomba, aceite de oliva virgen extra, sal, perejil fresco

Elaboración
Limpiar los chipirones, sacar la pluma y las tinta y rellenarlos con las patas, cerrar con un palillo para que no se salga. Salar y reservar.

Picar las cebollas y los ajos en trozos pequeños y pochar a fuego lento durante 15 minutos, agregar la salsa de tomate y los txipirones y dejar cociendo otros 15 o 20 minutos.

Pasar las tintas, que hemos extraido de los txipis, por un colador ayudándonos de un poco de salsa para que pasaen a la cazuela. Agregar la tinta de los sobres y cocinar durante otros 20 minutos hasta que la salsa espese.

Sacar los txipirones a un recipiente y triturar la salsa, pasarla por un chino y devolverla a la cazuela. Incorporar los txipirones otra vez y poner a punto de sal.

Elaborar un arroz blanco con una cucharada de aceite 2 dientes de ajo picados perejil y agua.

Presentar una base de arroz en el fondo y repartir los txipirones encima, salsear.

Lomo de Bonito al Romero

con Brandada de bacalao y cebolla confitada

Ingredientes

un lomo de bonito de 200 gr., 50 gramos de bacalao desalado, una patata mediana, 1 dl de leche, la pulpa de tres tomates, cebolla confitada crujiente, Aceite de oliva virgen extra, 1 diente de ajo, romero, sal y pimienta

Elaboración

Desalar el bacalao según instrucciones o se compra ya desalado. Escaldar durante 15 sg., secar y desmigar. En el mismo agua, cocer la patata, mientras freir el ajo laminado, escurrir y reservar. En un bol mezclar la patata, el bacalao y el ajo hasta formar un puré, al mismo tiempo se va echando el aceite y la leche, para que ligue con el puré. Reccificar de sal, echar un pelín de pimienta blanca.

Salpimentamos el lomo de bonito y lo salteamos con un poco de aceite de romero, durante 3 ó 4 minutos, marcándolo por todos los lados pero dejando el centro crudo.

En el plato echamos un chorrito de AOVE, con una cuchara extraemos un poco de pulpa del tomate y extendemos 2 cucharadas en el centro del plato, salpimentamos. cortamos una tajada de unos 2 cm de lomo de bonito y lo ponemos sobre el tomate con unas lascas de sal maldón. a un lado ponemos una buena cucharada de la brandada y espolvoreamos con la cebolla crujiente.

Txangurro
a la Donostiarra

Ingredientes

1 Centollo (de 1 kg.), 3 cucharadas de tomate, la parte blanca de medio puerro picado, media cebolla morada, 1 cucharada de mantequilla, 1 dl de brandy, 1 dl de AOVE, Pan rayado.

Elaboración

Picar muy fino la cebolla y el puerro. En una cazuela a fuego suave con una cucharada de aceite rehogar hasta que coja color, incorporar el tomate y dejar unos 15 minutos hasta que quede deshecho.

Mientras poner el centollo en agua este fría con sal, cuando hierva cocer 15 minutos. Abrir el txangurro, pasar el jugo por un colador fino. Sacar toda la carne de cuerpo y patas. Verter en la cazuela con la cebolla, el puerro y el tomate, agregar un chorrito de Brandy y mexclar bien todo. Dar un hervor de 2 minutos, probar el punto de sal.

Rellenar el caparazón del centollo con la mezcla, espolvorear por toda la superficie con pan rayado, poner unos trozos de mantequilla y gratinar 2 minutos.

Bacalao

Bacalao
a la Bizkaina

Ingredientes

Para 4 raciones, 4 lomos de bacalao desalado, 4 dientes de ajo, 4 dl. de aceite de oliva virgen, 2 puerros, 2 cebollas rojas, 2 cebollas blancas, 50 g. de jamón serrano, 3 ramas de perejil, costrones de pan tostado, la carne de 10 pimientos choriceros, 1 vasito de vino blanco, 1 chupito de Brandy, Pimienta blanca y Cayena.

Elaboración

Poner una cazuela, a fuego muy lento, con el aceite, los ajos y las cebollas picadas, los puerros, el jamón serrano, las ramas de perejil atadas, el vino blanco, el brandy y los costrones de pan. Dejar hacer suavemente durante 2 horas, hasta que quede dorado y deshecho. Quitar el jamón, el tocino y el perejil y agregar la pulpa de los choriceros, dejando hervir lentamente 15 minutos. El conjunto se pasa por el chino 4 veces.

Verter la salsa a una cazuela, poner a fuego lento, salpimentar. Dar un hervor de 5 minutos. Poner el bacalao con la piel hacia arriba en una cazuela de barro. Napar con la bizkaina y dejar que se temple a fugo medio bajo.

Bacalao

al Pil pil

Ingredientes

Para 4 raciones, 4 tajadas de bacalao desalado, 350 ml de Aceite de Oliva Virgen Extra, 4 dientes de ajo, 1 guindilla seca.

Elaboración

En una cazuela ponemos a calentar el aceite a fuego bajo, añadir los ajos, cuando cojan un color dorado los retiramos del fuego y dejamos 1/3 del aceite en la cazuela para que se atempere. Para esta receta vamos a trabajar con una temperatura entre 50 - 60 grados.

Introducimos las tajadas en la cazuela y la empezamos a menear con movimientos circulares. Poco a poco irá saliendo la gelatina del bacalao. Vamos incorporando el aceite reservado hasta que las tajadas emulsionen todo el líquido con la gelatina pero sin llegar a espesar demasiado.

Kokotxas y Carrilleras
al Pil pil

Ingredientes

250 gr de kokotxas de bacalao, 250 gr. de carrilleras de bacalao, 350 ml de Aceite de Oliva Virgen Extra, 4 dientes de ajo, 1 guindilla seca.

Elaboración

En una cazuela ponemos a calentar el aceite a fuego bajo, añadir los ajos, cuando cojan un color dorado los retiramos del fuego y dejamos 1/3 de aceite en la cazuela para que enfríe.

Sazonar y enharinar las kokotxas y las carrilleras, marcarlas vuelta y vuelta e introducimos en la cazuela y la empezamos a menear con movimientos circulares. Poco a poco irá saliendo la gelatina del bacalao. Vamos incorporando el aceite reservado hasta que las kokotxas y las emulsionen el aceite con la gelatina pero sin llegar a espesar mucho.

Decorar con los ajos.

Bacalao

Ajoarriero

Ingredientes

1,2 kg. de bacalao desalado, 3 cebolletas, La pulpa de 4 pimientos choriceros (50 g), 5 pimientos verdes, 300 g de tomate frito, 1 l. de aceite de oliva virgen extra, 4 dientes de ajo, Perejil picado, Sal.

Elaboración

Cortar los lomos de bacalao en tacos 200 g cada uno. Picar las cebolletas y los pimientos verdes y pocharlos en una cazuela con 200 g de aceite de oliva a fuego suave durante 20 minutos o hasta que esté bien hecho. Añadir la pulpa de pimiento choricero, el tomate frito y cocer durante otros 5 minutos poner a punto de sal y reservar caliente. En otra cazuela confitar el bacalao con el resto del aceite de oliva y los dientes de ajo pelados a fuego mínimo (50ºc) durante 8 a 15 minutos dependiendo del grosor del lomo del bacalao. Añadir el bacalao al sofrito. mezclando suavemente, calentar hasta que el calor entre en el bacalao, espolvorear con perejil picado y servir.

Zurrukutuna

ó sopa de ajo con bacalao

Ingredientes

200 g. de bacalao desmigado y desalado. 1 pan "zopako". 2 dl. de aceite de oliva virgen. 2 cabezas de ajo. 6 pimientos choriceros. 4 cucharadas de salsa de tomate, ½ guindilla seca. 4 huevos. Agua del desalado del bacalao.

Elaboración

Cocer en agua los pimientos choriceros separar de la piel y triturar. Cubrir justo el fondo de una cazuela de barro con aceite, cuando esté caliente echar el pan cortado en rodajas y tostar, pero sin quemar. Casi al final agregar el tercio de guindilla picada.

En otra cazuela de barro con un poco de aceite se echar los ajos picados, cuando empiecen a tomar color agregar el bacalao desalado y desmigado. A continuación, incorporar un poco del agua del desalado y ligar como si se tratase de un pil pil.

Incorporar a la cazuela del bacalao el pan tostado, los trocitos de guindilla y la pulpa de los pimientos choriceros. Añadir un poco más de agua del desalado y dejar hacer lentamente durante una media hora. Probar y rectificar de sal. Dejar reposar una hora.

Para 4 comensales, separar la clara de 4 huevos y batir a punto de nieve con un pellizco de sal. Por otro lado batir las yemas y unir poco a poco a las claras batidas.

Presentar en el plato una ración de zurrukutuna, con una cuchara napar la parte de arriba con la mezcla del huevo y quemar con un soplete hasta que adquiera un color tostado y haya cuajado, servir.

Bacalao

Club Ranero

Ingredientes

800 gr de bacalao, 3 dl de AOVE, 3 dientes de ajo, 1 cucharada de perejil picado, 50 gr de pimiento verde, 50 gr de pimiento rojo, 100 gr de cebolla morada de zalla.

Elaboración

Desalar el bacalao y quitar espinas, pelar y laminar los ajos (si tuviera gérmen eliminar), Picar la cebolla y los pimientos muy finos, pochar en una sartén y reservar.

Calentar una cazuela con el aceite de oliva y los ajos, cuando bailen en la superficie retirar. Introducir el bacalao, bajar la intensidad del fuego y comenzar movimientos de va y ven hasta conseguir ligar un pil pil ligero.

En el plato, presentar una cama de verduras pochadas, poner la tajada de bacalao encima, napar con el pil pil y espolvorear otro puñao de verduritas encima.

Brandada
de bacalao

Ingredientes

200 g. de bacalao desmigado y desalado. Aceite de oliva virgen extra. 2 cabezas de ajo. 2 patatas medianas,

Elaboración

Cocer en agua las patatas, pelar y trocear. Escaldar el bacalao durante 3 ó 4 minutos. Desmigar el bacalao.

Trituramos el bacalao las patatas y los ajos. Incorporamos un poco de agua de la coción del bacalao, batir agregando poco a poco el aceite de oliva como si estuvieramos montando una mayonesa.

Servir sobre tostadas de pan y aliñamos con un poco de aceite en crudio.

de alas y de patas

Pollo Relleno

Guisado a la cerveza

Ingredientes

1 pollo de corral deshuesado, 100 gr de carne picada, 25 gr de foie, 25 gramos de jamón serrano, 150 gr de seta de cardo, 2 huevos, 2 cerverzas (33cl), 1 cebolla roja, 1 pimiento verde, 4 dientes de ajo, romero, tomillo, orégano, aceite de oliva, sal y pimienta.

Elaboración

Deshuesar el pollo sin romper la piel para poder rellenarlo. En una sartén saltear el ajo, la cebolla y el pimiento todo muy picado, añadir el jamón, el foie la carne picada, el romero, el tomillo el orégano y salpimentar, cocinar hasta que el relleno esté hecho. En otra sartén saltear las setas picadas con un diente de ajo y agregar a la la mezcla del relleno. Reservar.

Salpimentar el pollo por dentro y por fuera, rellenar con la mezcla e introducir 2 huevos cocidos. Cerrar el pollo con palillos.

En una cazuela más alta que el pollo sofreir con 2 cucharadas de aceite: 2 dientes de ajo, 1 cebolla y 1 pimiento picados, cuando adquiera un color dorado, introducir el pollo, añadir las 2 cervezas y guisar durante 3/4 de hora a fuego 5/9, dándole la vuelta de vez en cuando. El líquido tiene que reducir a la mitad.

Triturar la salsa, servir el pollo en rodajas y napar con la salsa.

Cabrito asado
al Romero

Ingredientes

1/2 cabrito lechal, 6-8 patatas rojas, romero fresco, 2 hojas de laurel, sal gruesa, manteca de cerdo y un vaso de agua.

Elaboración

Salamos el cabrito, lo untamos con manteca de cerdo y el romero le damos un masaje por todas partes, y lo ponemos en la fuente de horno.

Lo asamos a 160 grados unas dos horas, dándole la vuelta cada 30 minutos para que se haga de forma homogénea. Cuando lleven una hora y las hayamos tenido asando durante media hora por cada lado, añadimos un chorrito de agua por encima.

Trans la segunda hora, el cabrito habrá tomado un pecioso color. Si fuera preciso, añadimos medio vaso de agua para terminar. El objetivo es obtener una intensa salsa que recogerá toda la sustancia del cabrito.

Parrilla Ibérica

Secreto, Pluma, Presa y Solomillo

Ingredientes

1 secreto ibérico, 1 presa ibérica, 1 pluma ibérica, 1 solomillo ibérico, 6-8 patatas rojas, romero fresco, 2 hojas de laurel, aceite de oliva, sal y pimienta.

Elaboración

Salpimentamos cada despiece, lo untamos aceite de oliva y el romero le damos un masaje por todas partes y dejamos que macere 1 ó 2 horas. Sellamos en una plancha o sartén, cada pieza, hasta que adquiera un ligero color dorado por todos los lados.

En una fuente de horno colocamos las piezas enteras, a 180 grados, hay que tener en cuenta los tiempos de coción en función del grosor de cada pieza. El secreto por ser más fino se cocerá antes y habrá que introducirlo más tarde, así todos los despieces tendrán igual punto de asado. Dejar reposar un par de minutos y cortar cada pieza en porciones.

Como guarnición unas patatas fritas ó una ensalada van perfectos.

Magret de Pato
en salsa de cítricos

Ingredientes

2 magrets de pato frescos, 100 ml de vino Pedro Ximénez, 1 cucharadita de maicena, 1 limón, 1 naranja, 80 g de Azúcar Moreno, Sal y Pimienta al gusto, Flor de sal o en su defecto sal gorda común, 2-3 ramitas de romero.

Elaboración

lavar la naranja y el limón, cortar la piel (sin lo blanco) en láminas muy finas. Escaldar en agua hirviendo 30 seg. y escrrir. Exprimir la fruta y colar el zumo. Verter el P.X. en un cazo, reducir durante 4 minutos, evaporando el alcohol. En el mismo cazo, agregar la piel de las frutas, el zumo y el azúcar moreno, dejar a fuego suave 2 minutos. Disolver la maicena con 2 cucharadas de agua fría. Añadir al cazo con la salsa así espesará un poco. Reserva la salsa.

Hacer cortes finos sobre la piel de los magrets en ambos sentidos, formando una rejilla, salpimentar bien. Dorar por la parte de la piel: a fuego fuerte hasta que la grasa se haya reducido a la mitad, bajar el fuego. Agregar el romero y dar la vuelta al magret en 5 minutos (al gusto). Dorar el otro lado 5 minutos más.

Cuando la carne esté al punto, cortar a lo ancho filetes de 1 1/2 cm. (1/2 magret por persona es una buena ración). Cubrir con la salsa y con un poco de flor de sal. Servir en plato caliente.

Puedes acompañar este plato con tomates confitados o una ensalada de queso, aguacate y uva.

Rabo de Toro

Guisado

Ingredientes

1,5 kg de rabo de toro, 1 puerro, 1 cebolla grande, 3 zanahorias, 1 pimiento rojo, 2 dientes de ajo, 750 ml de vino tinto, 1/2 l. de caldo de carne, 2 hojas de laurel, sal pimienta y harina.

Elaboración

Salpimentamos los trozos del *rabo de toro*. Enharinamos y doramos en una sartén o cazuela con 4 o 5 cucharadas de aceite de oliva. Cuando estén dorados, pochamos en ese mismo aceite el puerro, la cebolla, los ajos (pelados y enteros) y el pimiento rojo, limpios y cortados en trozos no muy grandes. Añadimos el laurel junto con las zanahorias limpias y en láminas. Dejamos unos minutos para que se ablanden las verduras. Sazonamos. Incorporamos los trozos del rabo de toro y cubrimos con el vino y el caldo. Cuando rompa el hervor, desespumamos, tapamos la cazuela y dejamos cocer a fuego lento unas tres horas. Probamos el punto de sal y que la carne esté tierna y hecha (se tiene que separar del hueso).

Sacamos los trozos del rabo de toro a una fuente de servir y pasamos la salsa por un chino. Nos tiene que quedar una salsa espesita y brillante (como la de la fotografía), si no tiene "consistencia" la ponemos a reducir en un cazo al fuego.

Cubrimos con la salsa y servimos como acompañamiento, si queremos, con unas patatas fritas ó una ensalada.

Carrillera Ibérica

Asada con pure de papas

Ingredientes

800 gr de carrilleras de cerdo ibérico, 3 patatas grandes, 1 puerro, 1 zanahoria, 1/2 cebolla morada, orégano, romero, AOVE, sal y pimienta.

Elaboración

Limpiamos las carrilleras de telillas, grasa y restos de despojos. Sazonar, aderezar con orégano, romero y un poco de AOVE. Introducimos en el horno precalentado a 180º, durante 1 hora, dándoles la vuelta a mitad de cocción.

Mientras rehogamos 1 diente de ajo, la cebolla, el puerro y la zanahoria con 3 cucharadas de AOVE. Sazonamos y dejamos que se dore moviéndolo de vez en cuando. Cubrimos con agua y dejamos cocer a fuego medio durante 20 minutos. Agregamos las patatas cocidas, trituramos, rectificamos de sal y reservar.

Servimos las carrilleras sobre el fondo de puré de patatas.

Txuletón
a la plancha

Ingredientes

1 Chuleta de vaca de 1,5 kg, sal en escama (maldón u otra similar)

Elaboración

La chuleta debe estar a temperatura ambiente una hora antes de hacerla. Poner la plancha en el fuego alto. Cuando alcance la temperatura ponemos el canto con la parte grasa, en un instante observaremos cómo la grasa derretida aparece en la plancha, es entonces cuando comenzamos a hacer la chuleta con su propia grasa, no necesita aceite.

El punto, en una chuleta con un grosor de unos 4 cm sería, 1 cm hecho por cada lado y 2 cm rojo en el centro.

Una vez asada la chuleta, es conveniente delarja reposar un par de minutos antes de cortar, pues se escaparía todo el jugo.

Se puede servir con unos pimientos de Gernika y unas patatas fritas.

y de postre...

Pantxineta

con crema pastelera

Ingredientes

2 placas de hojaldre, 1 huevo, 1 puñado de almendra crudaa fileteada,

Para la crema pastelera:
3 yemas de huevo, 1 huevo, 120 gr de azucar, 60 gramos de maizena y 1/2 litro de leche.

Elaboración

Comenzamos con la crema pastelera. Ponemos en un cazo el huevo, las 3 yemas, el azucar y batimos, añadimos la maizena y seguimos batiendo hasta que esté todo bien integrado. Agregamos la leche, seguimos batiendo hasta que quede bien mezclado. Llevamos el cazo al fuego(medio) y seguimos batiendo sin parar hasta que la crema espese, cuando haya cogido cuerpo, bajamos el fuego al mínimo y removemos 1 minuto más. Separamos del fuego y dejamos enfriar.

Cubrimos una bandeja de horno con papel sulfurizado y ponemos sobre ella una de las placas de hojaldre. echamos la crema pastelera y la extendemos bien por toda la superficie. Cubrimos con la segunda placa de hojaldre. Pintamos con huevo batido y ponemos almendra fileteada, bien repartida por la tarta.

Metemos al horno a 180º con calor arriba y abajo, durante 20 minutos. Hasta que coja color dorado.

Intxaursaltsa
crema de nueces

Ingredientes
1 litro de leche, 150 grs. de nueces molidas, 200 grs. de azúcar, 1 palito de canela.

Elaboración
En una cazuela ponemos la leche, las nueces y la canela y llevamos al fuego removiendo continuamente, tiene que espesar un poco y quedarse de "color marrón" sin dejar de remover con cuchara de madera. Cuando espese, añadimos el azúcar y se tiene un poco al fuego sin dejar de remover para que no se peguen las nueces a la cazuela. Debe quedar como una crema. Metemos al frigorífico y servimos en cazuelitas individuales, adornando con nueces o canela en polvo.

La intxaursalsa, es un postre navideño de hace más de 150 años, típico de los caseríos vascos ya que abundaban las nueces recogidas durante el otoño y la leche. Este postre casi desapareció de nuestras mesas y en los años ochenta los cocineros vascos lo rescataron de su olvido. Existen dos versiones, las dos dulces, una incorpora bacalao y la otra chocolate.

Leche frita

con azucar y canela

Ingredientes

400 gr de leche, 35 gr de maizena, 80 gr de azucar, la cáscara de un limón, un palo de canela, 2 huevos, canela en polvo.

Elaboración

Ponemos a infusionar en una cazuela 300 ml de leche el palo de canela, el azucar y la peladura del limón. Cuando llegue a evullición, apagar el fuego, tapar la cazuela y dejar reposar durante 15 minutos. Colamos la leche infusionada y la pasamos a un cazo limpio.

En los 100 ml de leche restantes, disolvemos la maizena y batimos enérgicamente. vertemos la mezcla sobre la leche infusionada y ponemos de nuevo al fuego bajo, removiendo constantemente hasta que se integren todos los ingredientes. Pasados 20 minutos, estará en su punto.

Volcamos la crema en una bandela rectangular y cubrimos con un film de cocina. Metemos a enfriar en la nevera de un día pa otro. Una vez fría, cortamos en cuadrados, las pasamos por harina, huevo y las freímos en aceite caliente, cuando estén doradas las escurrimos y las rebozamos en una mezcla de azucar y canela en polvo.

Adornamos con virutas de peladura de limón.

y de postre...

Arroz con leche

Pasas y canela

Ingredientes

300 gr de arroz redondo, 2 litros de leche entera, 2 palos de canela, peladura de limón, 150 gr de azucar blanco, 250 gramos de mantequilla y sal.

Elaboración

Lavar el arroz con abundante agua fría, para que pierda almidón y quede un grano más suelto. Meterlo en un cazo cubierto con agua y un pellizco de sal. Ponerlo a fuego lento hasta que hierva, retirar.

En otro cazo hervir la leche con las ramas de canela y la peladura del limón, cuando hierva sacamos la canela y la piel de limón, ponemos a fuego lento y añadimos el arroz escurrido y dejamos que cueza durante 1 hora.

10 minutos antes de que el arroz esté listo, añadimos el azucar y la mantequilla. Remover bien hasta que adquiera una textura cremosa. corregir de azucar si fuera necesario.

Servimos en cuencos individuales, espolvorear canela en polvo.

Torrijas
de leche y de vino

Ingredientes

Torrijas de leche:

Por cada 20 gr. de rebanada de pan, 1/2 cucharada de miel, 1 cucharada de aceite de oliva, 1/2 vaso de leche, 1/3 de huevo, azucar, canela y cáscara de limón (sólo la parte verde).

Torrijas de vino:

Por cada 20 gr. de rebanada de pan, 1/2 cucharada de miel, 1 cucharada de aceite de oliva, 1/4 vaso de lagua, 1/4 vaso de vino 1/3 de huevo, azucar, canela y cáscara de limón (sólo la parte verde)

Elaboración

Calentamos la leche y añadimos la miel. Dejamos que se enfríe un poco para que el pan no quede demasiado blando cuando las remojemos. Una vez remojadas las rebanadas de pan las pasamos por huevo batido y las freímos en aceite de oliva caliente. Las escurrimos bien y las ponemos en papel secante. Añadimos, por último la canela al gusto.

Calentamos el vino tinto junto al agua, la miel, y la cáscara de limón. Dejamos que hierva durante tres minutos para que el alcohol se evapore y dejamos que se enfríe. En una sartén calentamos el aceite de oliva y remojamos en el vino el pan durante unos segundos, escurrimos un poco y las rebozamos en el huevo batido antes de freírlaspor ambos lados. Las colocamos sobre papel absorbente para sacar el exceso de grasa. Añadir la canela al gusto.

Goxua

Ingredientes

Crema pastelera:
100 g de azúcar, 500 ml de leche, 50 g de maicena, 3 huevos.

Bizcochos de soletilla, Nata 35%, 30g azúcar lustre,

Almíbar:
6 cucharadas de agua por 6 cucharadas de azúcar y un chorrito de licor

Elaboración

Para la creama pastelera, trabajamos los huevos con el azúcar hasta obtener una mezcla fina, después añadimos la maicena y finalmente añadimos la leche caliente que podemos haber aromatizado con canela o vainilla y no paramos de remover hasta que hierva. Entonces lo sacamos del fuego y seguimos removiendo un rato más. Enfriar y reservar.

Montamos la nata con las varillas añadiendo unos 30 g de azúcar lustre. Reservamos

Hacemos un almíbar con el azúcar, el agua y el licor elegido calentándolo en el fuego. En este almíbar, una vez frío, mojamos los bizcochos.

Para montar el plato, en un vaso ancho se monta, primero la nata, luego los bizcochos y finalmente la crema pastelera para finalmente adornarlo con caramelo ó azucar quemado con un soplete.

Queso
membrillo y nueces

Ingredientes

Propuesta de Tabla de quesos:

D.O. del Roncal (Navarra)
D.O. Idiazabal (Navarra-EH)
D.O. Arribes (Salamanca
D.O. la Mancha (Castilla-La Mancha)

Elaboración

Si hay un postre típico en Euskadi, ese es el queso con membrillo y nueces. Pocas cosas hay más sencillas, sin ningún tipo de elaboración, pero está tan rico que pocos vascos nos resistimos a sus encantos. Te cortan una cuña de queso Idiazabal ahumado en lonchas, acompañado de unas barras de dulce de membrillo y un canasto de nueces con el abridor.... y allí te las compongas. Y si lo acompañas de un vaso de vino tinto, ya oímos hasta campanas celestiales. Es un postre muy habitual en la sidrerías, escoltando una tortilla de bacalao, un buen txuletón a la brasa y claro está regado con txotx (toda la sidra que seas capaz de ingerir), pero para el postre, se suele pedir una botella de vino, para acompañar esta delicatessen tan nuestra. El poderoso sabor de un queso Idiazabal ahumado, junto a unas ricas y sanas nueces de caserío y el punto dulce del membrillo. Yo esta vez os lo presento en forma de una especie de gnoquis, los tres ingredientes convertidos en masa y rebozados en polvo de nueces machacadas

Sorbete de Manzana

dulce de membrillo y nueces

Ingredientes

Para el sorbete:

900 gr de manzana granny smith, el zumo de 2 limones, 570 gr de almibar de canela y una pizca de sal.

Para el almibar:

350 gr de azucar, media rama de canela, 350 cl de agua, una pizca de sal y el zumo de un limón.

Para edecorarar:

100 gr de nueces picadas, Caramelo líquido y dulce de membrillo.,

Elaboración

Un día antes ponemos el azúcar, la canela, la pizca de sal y el agua en un **cazo**. Llevar a ebullición y lo dejar hervir 3 minutos a fuego alto. Agregar el zumo del limón y lo dejar reposar hasta el día siguiente en un tarro.

Lavar y descorazonar las manzanas sin quitar la piel. Trocearlas y guardarlas en un cuenco con agua y el zumo de los limones para que no se oxiden. Triturar junto con el almibar y la sal hasta lograr un pure muy fino (cuanto más fino sea mejor quedará el sorbete).

Pasar el pure por un colador y echar en la máquina heladora. Si no se dispone de heladora. Poner el pure en un recipiente ancho y con poca altura. meter en el congelador, sacar ca hora y remover hasta conseguir la textura de sorbete.

Para la presentación ponemos en el fondo de una copa tipo Cocktail, un poco de dulce de membrillo. Mezclar una cantidad de sorbete con 1 yogurt natural batir hasta lograr una textura cremosa. Agregar a cada copa la crema, dejando sin cubrir un centímetro, Espolvorear unas nueces trituradas y decorar con caramelo líquido.

unos vinos...

Muga

Bodega Muga S.L. Haro (La Rioja)
D.O. Rioja
http://www.bodegasmuga.com

Uva:

Tempranillo 70%, Garnacha 20%, Mazuelo 7%, Graciano 3%.

Crianza:

24 meses en barricas hechas con robles seleccionados en tonelería propia. Clarificado con claras de huevos frescos.

Tono:

Capa media-alta de rojo brillante muy puro, casi monocromo. Nariz muy frutal con notas florales. Encontramos mermelada de guinda fresca, compota de frutillos, algo de regaliz, planta de anís, notas de hinojo y flor blanca. La boca es suave, con dominancia de taninos muy redondos y dulces, sorprendente teniendo en cuenta la edad del vino. Acidez natural presente pero difuminada que no molesta en absoluto.

Alcohol:

14% vol.

Temperatura:

Servir entre los 16 y 18º.

Viña Tondonia 2001

R. Lopez de Heredia Viña Tondonia
Haro (La Rioja)
D.O. Rioja
http://www.lopezdeheredia.com

Uva:

Tempranillo 75%, Garnacha 15%, Mazuelo y Graciano 10%.

Crianza:

6 años en toneles de roble, sometido a 2 trasiegos. Clarificaión con huevos frescos.

Tono:

Rubí brillante con ligeros ribetes teja. Nariz: Nariz muy fina, fresca, tostada con ligeros aromas a vainilla. Muy persistente. Gusto: Muy seco, suave, redondo y desarrollado.

Alcohol:

14% vol.

Temperatura:

Servir entre los 18 y 20º.

Remelluri

Granja de Ntra Señora de Remelluri
La Bastida (La Rioja)
D.O. Rioja
http://www.remelluri.com

Uva:

Tempranillo 90%, Garnacha 5%, Graciano 5%.

Crianza:

18 meses en barricas de roble.

Tono:

Color cereza picota de muy buena intensidad. Borde granate. Rico en aromas de primera nariz intensos, negros minerales y carnosos. Fondo a hierbas aromáticas, monte bajo y sotobosque, seguido de aromas de farándanos y grosellas confitadas. En boca des de ataque redondo, cálido y elegante. Magnífica sensación tánica , paso sabroso suculento y persistente.

Alcohol:

13% vol.

Temperatura:

Servir entre los 16 y 18º.

Tempranillo 75%, Garnacha 10%,
Mazuelo 10%.

Crianza:

16 meses en barrica bordelesa de roble francés y americano con 4 trasiegos.

Tono:

Rojo cereza intenso, aromas de crianza con matices especiados. En boca vigoroso, estructurado y amplio, con taninos nobles bien conjuntados y largos. De final largo y consistente.

Alcohol:

14% vol.

Temperatura:

Servir entre los 16 y 18º.

Mesopotamia

Abadia de Aribayos (Zamora)
D.O. Arribes
http://clubmesopotamia.com/index.php

Uva:

Juan García

Crianza:

12 meses en barricas de roble francés.
Fue el 1° Vino elaborado dentro de la D.O. Arribes, en Fermoselle, lugar en el que se unen el Río Duero y el Tormes, de ahí el nombre del vino. Mesopotamia significa "Entre dos aguas".

Tono:

Rojo intenso de capa alta, lágrima densa y tintada, brillante. Aromas de guindas en licor, terroso, mineral, trufa, humo, ahumado. En boca es potente, carnoso, envolvente y de buena estructura, terminada con un postgusto a mermelada de moras.

Alcohol:

13,5% vol.

Temperatura:

Servir entre los 16 y 18°C.

El Secreto del Vettón

Cooperativa Arribes de Duero
Corporario (Salamanca)
D.O. Arribes
http://www.bodegasarribesdelduero.com

Uva:

Bruñal

Crianza:

29 meses en barricas de roble francés y americano.

Tono:

Color cereza picota de muy buena intensidad. Borde granate. Rico en aromas de primera nariz intensos, negros minerales y carnosos. Fondo a hierbas aromáticas, monte bajo y sotobosque, seguido de aromas de farándanos y grosellas confitadas. En boca des de ataque redondo, cálido y elegante. Magnífica sensación tánica , paso sabroso suculento y persistente.

Alcohol:

13% vol.

Temperatura:

Servir entre los 16 y 18º.

Arribes de Vettonia

Vendimia Seleccionada
Bodegas Arribes (Corporario) Salamanca
D.O. Arribes
http://www.bodegasarribesdelduero.com

Uva:

Bruñal

Crianza:

24 meses en barrica de roble francés y americano.

Tono:

Rojo rubí con algunas tonalidades teja en capa fina. Escelente brillo en un vino que no ha sido filtrado ni clarificado y que demiestra el cuidado exquisito de la crianza en barrica. En nariz de gran complejidad, donde se encuentran perfectamente ensamblados unos pequeños toques frutales a zarzamora y frutas negras del bosque muy maduras, con balsámicos. En boca aterciopelado, muy suave y envolvente, con un paladar rico y el toque preciso de los recuerdos varietales, dando un vino de gran persistencia.

Alcohol:

13% vol.

Temperatura:

Servir entre los 17 y 18º.

Gran Abadengo

Bodegas Bodegas Ribera de Pelazas
Pereña (Salamanca)
D.O. Arribes
http://www.bodegasriberadepelazas.com/
RiberaPelazas

Uva:

Juan García

Crianza:

Fermentado en tanques de madera
18 meses en barricas de roble frances y rumano

Tono:

Rojo cereza intenso, aromas de crianza con matices especiados. En boca vigoroso, estructurado y amplio, con taninos nobles bien conjuntados y largos. De final largo y consistente.

Alcohol:

14% vol.

Temperatura:

Servir entre los 16 y 18º.

Egia Enea

Bodega bizkai barne
Orozko (Bizkaia)
D.O. Bizkaiko Txakoliña
D.O. Arribes
http://bizkaikotxakolina.eus/bodegas/bodega-bizkai-barne/

Uva:

70% Hondarribi zuri zerratia, 30% Hondarribi zuri

Matices:

Este Txakolí se elabora con las piezas más maduras del viñedo Egia Enea de Balmaseda. Su crianza en lías refuerza su carácter graso y maduro. Ofrece a la vista un color pajizo. En nariz, es un vino complejo con matices de fruta madura blanca y vegetales sobre un fondo de lías minerales. En boca, es un vino fresco y vivo gracias a su buena acidez.

Alcohol:

13% vol.

Temperatura:

Servir entre los 8 y 10°C.

Txabarri

Bodegas Txabarri. Zalla (Bizkaia)
D.O. Bizkaiko Txakolina
http://www.txakolitxabarri.com/

Uva:

Hondarribi zuri 80%, Riesling 10%, Saivignon blanc 10%.

Matices:

Amarillo claro con tonos verdosos. Limpio y de mucho brillo. En nariz, de intenso aroma de fruta de hueso y ligero toque cítrico. En boca, Ligero con pellizco carbónico, afrutado y de final ácido agradable.

Alcohol:

12,5% vol.

Temperatura:

Servir entre los 6 y 8º.

Premios:

Baco de Plata a la cosecha 2014. XXIX concurso nacional de vinos jóvenes.

1º Premio al txakolí blanco en la feria del último lunes de Gernika 2015.

Itsasmendi 7

Bodega Itsasmendi. Gernika (Bizkaia)
D.O. Bizkaiko txakolina

Uva:

Hondarribi zuri zerratie 70%, Riesling 17%, Hondarribi zuri13%

Matices:

Amarillo dorado con reflejos verdosos. En nariz intenso y rico en toques salinos y ahumados, frutos secos, fruta blanca y cítrica, ligeros anisados. En boca, buena sensación de untusidad, con una acidez perfectamente integrada, mucho volumen y estructura.

Alcohol:

13% vol.

Temperatura:

Servir entre los 8 y 10°C.

Premios:

Medalla de Oro en el Concurso Mundial de Bruselas 2014, a la Cosecha de 2012.

Bacchus Plata 2014

Bacchus de Oro 2012

Lightning Source UK Ltd.
Milton Keynes UK
UKRC021138101019
351329UK00005B/154